Empowering People through Encounter

ENACTING CATHOLIC SOCIAL TRADITION

Empowering People through Encounter

Catholic Social Teaching and Community Organizing

Erin Brigham
and
Maureen H. O'Connell

LITURGICAL PRESS
Collegeville, Minnesota

litpress.org

Cover design by Rosemary Strohm. Cross illustration courtesy of Getty Images.

Scripture quotations are from New Revised Standard Version Bible: Catholic Edition © 1989, 1993 National Council of the Churches of Christ in the United States of America. Used by permission. All rights reserved worldwide.

© 2025 by Erin Brigham and Maureen H. O'Connell
Published by Liturgical Press, Collegeville, Minnesota. All rights reserved. No part of this book may be used or reproduced in any manner whatsoever, except brief quotations in reviews, without written permission of Liturgical Press, Saint John's Abbey, PO Box 7500, Collegeville, MN 56321-7500. Printed in the United States of America.

ISBN: 979-8-4008-0097-9 979-8-4008-0098-6 (e-book)

Library of Congress Cataloging in Publication Control Number: 2025017556.

Contents

Introduction   1

Chapter One
    The Orienting Ethos of Encounter and One-to-Ones   11

Chapter Two
    Human Dignity and the Person as Protagonist   28

Chapter Three
    Solidarity and Power   43

Chapter Four
    Subsidiarity and Creating Pathways to Collective Power   58

Chapter Five
    The Common Good and Becoming a People
    Who Go Public with Faith   78

Conclusion
    Synodality and the Future
    of Catholic Community Organizing   101

Acknowledgments   115

Appendix   117

Bibliography   119

Introduction

When we were invited to contribute to this series on Catholic Social Thought (CST) in practice, we first turned to professional community organizers working in Catholic contexts to gauge interest and need in a book on CST[1] and organizing. Responses confirmed and amplified some of our initial observations. The praxis of relational organizing embodies the Catholic Social Tradition and could be better known and appreciated among parishioners, church leaders, and in classrooms teaching CST. Community organizers working in Catholic contexts find that the Catholic Social Tradition is not well-known and is an under-utilized tool for connecting faith and action. Finally, empowering Catholic organizers with the language and knowledge of their own tradition will equip them to engage the church on all levels and mobilize Catholics to enact social change. Therefore, we hope this book will be useful and enriching for organizers in Catholic communities as well as students of Catholic Social Thought who may or may not be familiar with the inspiring field of community organizing.

Because we want to center the voices of organizers in this book, we sent a qualitative, short-answer survey to ninety registrants in a February 2023 conference on community organizing and Catholic

---

[1] We use the language of Catholic Social Teaching, Catholic Social Thought, and Catholic Social Tradition throughout the book and use the abbreviation CST inclusively. We understand the Catholic Social Tradition to include Catholic Social Teaching (magisterial teaching) as well as the actions and ideas of others who have shaped the tradition. As we explain below, this book focuses on the contributions of community organizers to the Catholic Social Tradition.

Social Thought. We gathered fourteen responses from organizers, lay and ordained ministers, and academics connected to the field of community organizing that helped us structure the book in a way that would be helpful for two primary audiences: organizers working in Catholic contexts and students and practitioners of CST. Each person who responded to the survey volunteered to participate in a semi-structured interview in which we asked specific questions about the connection between faith, organizing, and the Catholic Social Tradition.[2]

In this book series on the Catholic Social Tradition in practice, we will highlight core themes of Catholic Social Thought as expressed in organizing practices. We are convinced that learning about organizing—better yet, practicing organizing—makes the Catholic Social Tradition real and relevant in a particularly powerful way. As scholars of CST, we recognize ways that community organizing has been critical in the development of the Catholic Social Tradition and embodies core principles of Catholic Social Teaching, including human dignity, solidarity, the common good, and subsidiarity. Before we dive into specific organizing practices, we want to clarify what we mean by community organizing.

What Do We Mean by Community Organizing?

Speaking to the 2015 World Meeting of Popular Movements in Bolivia, Pope Francis proclaimed, "[T]he future of humanity does not lie solely in the hands of great leaders, the great powers and the elites. It is fundamentally in the hands of peoples and in their ability to organize."[3] In fact, history validates the pope's sentiment. Organizing has been a core part of social movements across contexts, from workers organizing themselves for better wages and labor conditions to women and people of color organizing them-

---

[2] Survey questions and interview questions are available in the appendix.
[3] Pope Francis, "Address, Participation at the Second World Meeting of Popular Movements," July 9, 2015.

selves for civil rights. While diverse in forms and aims, organizing comes down to individuals forming a more powerful community to participate in building a common good that includes them and their interests.[4]

In the late 1930s and 1940s, a Chicago-based social analyst and activist named Saul Alinsky (1909–1972) articulated a vision and identified practices that laid the foundation for modern-day community organizing.[5] Alinsky was deeply connected to a particular neighborhood, Back of the Yards of Chicago, which, at the time, lacked many material resources but was rich in relationships, particularly those rooted in local congregations. Alinsky recognized the untapped power of these communities to enact social change and address the economic and political problems the neighborhood was facing. In 1939 Alinsky helped establish the Back of the Yards Neighborhood Council, through which organizations would come together to build power through relationships and identify and form community leaders. This laid the foundation for what is now described as broad-based organizing, characterized by the formation of coalitions that transcend single issues.[6]

It is worth noting here that Alinsky, of Jewish background and identity, was organizing among a majority Catholic neighborhood and collaborated closely with Catholic leaders who were working on anti-poverty efforts locally and nationally. His emphasis on human dignity, solidarity, and the common good represents Catholic

---

[4] Scholar of religion and politics Jeffrey Stout recognizes organizing as a fundamental expression of democratic political engagement and he observes that face-to-face encounters at the heart of organizing are "essential components of each of the major democratic reform movements in U.S. history." See Jeffrey Stout, *Blessed Are the Organized: Grassroots Democracy in America* (Princeton, NJ: Princeton University Press, 2010), 148.

[5] Alinsky wrote two foundational books on community organizing: *Reveille for Radicals* (Chicago: University of Chicago Press, 1945) and *Rules for Radicals: A Practical Primer for Realistic Radicals* (New York: Vintage Books, 1972).

[6] Richard L. Wood and Brad R. Fulton, *A Shared Future: Faith-Based Organizing for Racial Equity and Ethical Democracy* (Chicago: University of Chicago Press, 2015), chap. 1.

Social Teaching in a profound way.[7] The connection to faith was made more explicit by subsequent community organizers who developed, critiqued, and expanded Alinsky's legacy through various approaches and networks.

For example, the Industrial Areas Foundation (IAF), established by Alinsky in 1940, took shape under the subsequent leadership of Edward Chambers, followed by Ernesto Cortez. Departing from the more secular approach of Alinsky, these leaders recognized the power of shared narratives and shared values that motivate religious communities.[8] On the West Coast, a Jesuit priest named John Baumann, SJ, launched the Pacific Institute for Community Organization (PICO) in 1972, which is now Faith in Action, an interfaith community organizing network with a global presence. Today, the IAF and Faith in Action along with Gamaliel and DART (Direct Action Research Training Center) are the most prominent, though not exhaustive, community organizing networks that train professional organizers and empower local leaders through organizing.

While diverse in approach, these networks share characteristics that are essential to faith-based community organizing, which is the focus of this book. Faith-based community organizing relies on partnerships with congregations of varying faith traditions, differentiating it from other forms of organizing, which may embrace similar strategies. However, most faith-based community organizers increasingly not only partner with congregations but with other institutions such as schools, neighborhood associations,

---

[7] On Alinsky's relationship with the Catholic Church and particularly his influence on the formation of the US Catholic Bishops' Campaign for Human Development, see Lawrence Engel, "The Influence of Saul Alinsky on the Campaign for Human Development," *Theological Studies* 59 (1998): 636–61. On the ways Alinsky's organizing practices enact Catholic Social Teaching, see Nicholas Hayes-Mota, "Embodying the Common Good: Community Organizing as Practice and Tradition," *The Journal of Catholic Social Thought* 21, no. 2 (2024).

[8] Luca Ozzano and Sara Fenoglio, "Conceptions of Power and Role of Religion in Community Organising," *Religions* 13, no. 9 (2022): 1–16.

and labor unions.[9] Organizers work with congregations to identify and form leaders from within the community. They prioritize face-to-face encounters as a foundation for a relational culture. Building on relationships of trust, communities are empowered to identify their interests and employ strategies to promote these interests through democratic participation. This book will describe many of these strategies and practices of organizing as a way to illustrate the core principles of Catholic Social Thought.

What Do We Mean by CST?

Broadly speaking, the Catholic Social Tradition includes the thoughts and actions of the Catholic Church as it has responded to social issues throughout history. The tradition is rooted in the scriptural mandate to love God through loving one's neighbor, particularly the vulnerable, excluded, and oppressed. Catholics have interpreted and lived out the love of neighbor in different ways throughout history– from charitable works to social justice advocacy to community organizing. Advocacy, like community organizing, aims to transform unjust social, political, and economic structures by using one's voice, and often one's privilege, to enact change. One way to conceptualize the difference between advocacy and organizing is that organizing starts with building relationships, capacity, and voice of a community so that they can enact change through collective power.

The Catholic Social Tradition includes an official body of church teaching, originating with Pope Leo XIII's encyclical *Rerum Novarum* (1891), which reflects on the realities of workers that emerged during the Industrial Revolution. Subsequent documents, mostly papal encyclicals, have built upon this text, signaling a documentary tradition, marked by continuity and development. Recurring themes

---

[9] For more on the terminology of faith-based, congregation-based, and broad-based organizing as well as the shape of community organizing today, see Wood and Fulton, *Shared Future*, chap. 1.

6 *Empowering People through Encounter*

and principles—human dignity, common good, solidarity, subsidiarity—are observable throughout the church's social teaching. However, the scope and applications of these core themes have developed as the church has responded to the signs of the times, or social questions that mark each historical moment.

In this book, we refer to Catholic Social Thought (CST) in the broad sense of the living Catholic Social Tradition unless we specify Catholic Social Teaching, which points to the writings of church leaders. We understand these expressions of CST to be inseparable as the tradition has developed through a dynamic interplay of Catholics putting their faith in action and church leaders issuing statements and documents on the same social realities. For example, when Leo XIII wrote *Rerum Novarum*, socially-minded Catholics like German Archbishop Wilhelm Emmanuel von Kettler were already reflecting on the condition of work in light of the Christian faith and speaking out against the exploitation of workers. Similarly, *Gaudium et Spes* ("Pastoral Constitution on the Church in the Modern World"), one of the documents from the Second Vatican Council (1962–65), reflects the social movements working toward civil rights and peace and also inspired Catholic individuals and communities with its teaching.[10]

Recognizing the dynamic, bottom-up way the CST has developed creates space to recognize the contributions of community organizers to shaping and passing on the Catholic Social Tradition. The church's strong commitment to organized labor, enshrined in *Rerum Novarum* (1891), *Quadragesimo Anno* (1931), and *Laborem Exercens* (1981), reflects the work of labor priests like George Higgins and well-known Catholic organizers like Cesar Chavez and Dolores Huerta. Catholic teaching on peace and nonviolence, championed by Pope John XXIII in the 1960s and Pope Francis

---

[10] For a detailed history on how CST developed from the bottom-up as well as top-down, see Marvin Krier Mich, *Catholic Social Teaching and Movements* (Mystic, CT: Twenty-Third Publications, 1998, 6th printing 2006).

in the present day, reflects the thought and action of Dorothy Day and other Catholics who organized through nonviolent action.

This legacy continues in the work of many community organizers working in Catholic settings. At the same time, Catholic Social Teaching remains an underutilized resource for uniting and mobilizing Catholics in a politically divided society and church. Catholic Social Teaching has been described as the church's "best kept secret." This observation, made by Edward DeBerri and James Hug in 1985 still resonates with many people today.

In addition to the challenge of people not knowing about the rich social tradition of the church, there is another challenge we want to name. Pope Francis described resistance to the social message of the church, even among Catholics. Referring to the social teaching of the church, Pope Francis stated:

> [W]e find principles such as the preferential option for the poor, the universal destination of goods, solidarity, subsidiarity, participation, and the common good. These are all ways in which the Good News of the Gospel takes concrete form on a social and cultural level. And it saddens me that some members of the Church get annoyed when we mention these guidelines that belong to the full tradition of the Church. But the Pope must not stop mentioning this teaching, even if it often annoys people, because what is at stake is not the Pope but the Gospel.[11]

Pope Francis's observation clarifies the challenge of integrating CST fully into the life of the church. The challenge is not simply a lack of knowledge of CST but resistance to its demands. Meeting this challenge not only requires raising awareness but also agitating the status quo. Not surprisingly, Pope Francis turned to organizers in this endeavor. By gathering leaders of popular movements, many of whom would consider themselves to be organizers,

---

[11] Pope Francis, "Video Message of the Holy Father Francis on the Occasion of the Fourth World Meeting of Popular Movements," October 16, 2021.

Francis centered their voices in the church's social mission. Describing popular movements as "social poets," he recognized their creativity and ability to engender hope in the midst of social injustice. Describing them as "collective Samaritans," he affirmed their witness to the gospel through their proximity to the poor and oppressed.[12] Recognizing their resistance to a throw away culture that destroys life, Francis embraced organizers as co-conspirators in centering the gospel despite those who are annoyed with its prophetic message.

In fact, Pope Francis invited the entire church, the people of God, to be protagonists in the ongoing life of the church. Building upon a rich tradition of synodality, Francis evoked a synod on the family (2015), on young people (2018), and on the Amazonian region (2019). The Synod on Synodality, convened in 2021, implicitly evokes Francis's affinity for community organizing given its culminating focus on cultivating co-responsibility among all of the baptized for the church's mission. During this global synod, the church has witnessed people come together across identities, theologies, and political views to discern how the Spirit is leading the church today. Not only have church leaders relied concretely on the skills of community organizers to advance this work,[13] the ethos of synodality as a quality of the church affirms the importance of encounter, deep listening, and relational organizing in the church's social mission.

What to Expect from This Book

There are multiple lists of core principles of CST. Widely used in books on CST, the United States Conference of Catholic Bishops (USCCB) offers a comprehensive list: human dignity, the dignity

---

[12] Pope Francis, "Video Message, Fourth World Meeting of Popular Movements."

[13] Katie Collins Scott, "For Synod Listening Sessions, US Bishops Turned to Community Organizers," *National Catholic Reporter* (January 3, 2023).

of work and rights of workers, solidarity, the preferential option for the poor, rights and responsibilities, the call to community and participation, and the care for creation.[14] We kept these principles in mind as we structured the book around the principles listed in the *Compendium of the Social Doctrine of the Church*: human dignity, common good, solidarity, and subsidiarity. Each of these principles is paired with an organizing practice as a way to demonstrate the meaning and practical application of the principle and as a way to understand the components of community organizing.

Chapter 1 begins with the foundational practice of community organizing: the relational meeting or one-to-one. This practice illustrates the power of encounter to enact personal and social transformation, which Pope Francis repeatedly emphasized in his words and actions. We introduce the concept of encounter not as an additional principle of CST but as a lens that Pope Francis offered to us to illuminate the social tradition. For many organizers, the one-to-one is not only practical and effective, it is a spiritual practice that enables them to encounter the sacred dignity of each person.

Chapter 2 focuses on the principle of human dignity, foundational to Catholic Social Teaching. Specifically, we illustrate the following dimensions of human dignity: rights, conscience, and subjectivity in Catholic theology and social teaching. This principle shows up in organizing particularly through the practice of sharing one's story and listening deeply to the story of another person. The organizer does not create human dignity nor are they a passive observer of its power. Rather, as people who believe in the transformative power of storytelling, they shine a spotlight on human dignity and witness people step into their own protagonism.

Chapter 3 invites the reader to consider power from the perspective of a community organizer. In this context, power is understood

---

[14] United States Conference of Catholic Bishops, "Seven Themes of Catholic Social Teaching," drawn from *Sharing Catholic Social Teaching: Challenges and Directions* (Washington, DC: USCCB Publishing, 1998).

as an essential resource for a community to reach their goals. People acting together in solidarity builds power. This chapter will explore the meaning of solidarity in CST with particular attention to the scriptural mandate to solidarity with those who are vulnerable and oppressed. Christological and ecclesiological insights of liberation theology will reinforce this aspect of CST.

Chapter 4 continues our reflection on power by highlighting concrete practices through which organizers generate pathways to power. Specifically, it describes the practices of a listening campaign, research action meetings, mapping assets, cutting an issue, and agitation. It highlights subsidiarity as a moral, political and ecclesial principle, reinforcing the connection between organizing, CST, and synodality.

Chapter 5 describes the common good in CST, including its theological dimensions and political implications. Organizers build up the common good by generating imagination of the world as it should be and by holding institutions accountable to this vision. In doing so, they demonstrate the public implications of faith convictions and incorporate strategies for engaging a pluralistic public sphere. Finally, the chapter presents organizing as a critically needed conduit for generating the common good in a polarized church and society.

Far from abstract, these core principles of CST are learned and applied through practice. The practices of community organizing offer a particularly compelling way to encounter the Catholic Social Tradition. Throughout this text you will hear the stories of organizers who have all, in various ways, advanced the common good through solidarity and a resolute belief in the sacred dignity of each person. Listening to the ways they experienced a call to organize, were transformed by one-to-one meetings, and found consolation in solidarity with others has convinced us of the power of encounter.

Chapter ONE

The Orienting Ethos of Encounter and One-to-Ones

Describing why she became an organizer, Lucia points to the faith of people she has met in the work. "I encounter God every single day throughout the day because of encountering people [for whom] nothing but faith can help them get up in the morning . . . " She spoke specifically of migrants who are organizing to improve their communities, schools, and working conditions. As an immigrant from Central America, she identifies with this community. Their witness has ignited her own faith, which had been dormant inside her despite being Catholic all of her life.

Reflecting on her faith, she talked about feeling disconnected and disappointed in the Catholic Church because of its historical connection to the colonization of Latin America. With her passion for social justice, she became a union organizer but initially resisted organizing with churches. Then she met a charismatic deacon who was organizing in Catholic parishes. Working with him helped her see the power of congregation-based organizing and changed her perspective on the church. Through organizing with faith communities, she encountered and experienced the church as the people of God, which has renewed her own faith. Still, she said, "I cannot tell you [that] I encounter God in the church . . . . But I love going to church with people." She especially finds God "in the faces of people that find the courage to, you know, confront reality and do it courageously."[1]

This story illustrates the power of face-to-face encounter to enact personal transformation. In fact, the history of community organizing is full of these stories, which collectively demonstrate the power of person-to-person encounter to enact societal and ecclesial transformation. Experienced organizers told us that one-to-ones, also called relational meetings, are foundational to their work. One reason for this is practical: people, far more than ideas or issues, inspire commitment and collective action. However, in speaking with faith-driven organizers like Lucia, we have heard another reason the one-to-one is foundational. For them, it is a spiritual practice, an opportunity to encounter God reflected in the dignity of the person.

In this chapter, we will explore the theological underpinnings of encounter in the thought of Pope Francis. By emphasizing encounter, Francis brought a particularly relational, person-centered lens to the Catholic Social Tradition (CST), which we will highlight in the pages that follow. By starting with the concept of encounter, we do not intend to introduce it as an additional theme of CST (along with human dignity, the common good, etc.) but rather as a lens that illuminates CST in a particularly relational and transformative way. Perhaps not surprisingly, Francis turned to leaders of popular movements, many of whom are organizers, as agents of hope, models of Christian discipleship, and sources of ecclesial renewal. To better understand the transformative power of encounter, we will examine the practice of the one-to-one, which has been described and analyzed by several organizers and scholars.[2] Then, we will offer some insights on the theological and spiritual dimen-

---

[1] Names have been changed to protect anonymity. Interview with Lucia, October 17, 2023.

[2] See Stout, *Blessed Are the Organized*; Aaron Stauffer, "The Relational Meeting as a Political and Religious Practice," *Political Theology* 23, nos. 1–2 (2022) 167–73; Dennis Jacobsen, *Doing Justice: Congregations and Community Organizing,* 2nd ed. (Minneapolis: Fortress Press, 2017); and Gordan Whitman, *Stand*

sions of the one-to-one before exploring how this relational practice creates possibilities for social and ecclesial change.

Starting with Encounter

Encounter is a central theme in the theological and social vision of Pope Francis. By studying the writings of Jorge Bergoglio, the Argentinian Jesuit who became Pope Francis, scholars have identified four recurring themes. These "Bergoglian principles" include: time is greater than space, realities are greater than ideas, unity prevails over conflict, and the whole is greater than the part (*Evangelii Gaudium* 217–37). These principles, developed not only through his intellectual formation, which was shaped in a significant way by the dialectical philosophy of Romano Guardini, but also through his personal and pastoral experiences, give a particular shape to Francis's teachings.[3] His attentiveness to concrete realities, historical context, and unity in diversity are captured in the theme of encounter, making this a defining feature of Francis's social thought.

Encounter, for Pope Francis, is an essential dimension of the human experience. In fact, Francis believes that we cannot know ourselves "apart from an encounter with other persons" (*Fratelli Tutti* 87). With a pronounced emphasis, Francis also affirms a core tenant of Catholic thought: that people are inherently relational and that our innate dignity is realized in and through community. Francis captures the theological dimension behind this anthropology in his 2013 apostolic exhortation, *Evangelii Gaudium* ("The Joy of the Gospel"). In it, he assumes that our primary experience of encounter is with God. This experience is foundational to our

---

Up! How to Get Involved, Speak Out, and Win in a World on Fire (Oakland, CA: Berrett-Koehler Publishers, 2018).

[3] Ethna Regan, "The Bergoglian Principles: Pope Francis' Dialectical Approach to Political Theology," *Religions* 10, no. 12 (2019): 670; and Juan Carlos Scannone, "Pope Francis and the Theology of the People," *Theological Studies* 77, no. 1 (March 2016).

capacity for self-transcendence and meaningful relationships with others. Francis explains,

> Thanks solely to this encounter—or renewed encounter—with God's love, which blossoms into an enriching friendship, we are liberated from our narrowness and self-absorption. We become fully human when we become more than human, when we let God bring us beyond ourselves in order to attain the fullest truth of our being. (8)

While it is essential to the human experience, it extends beyond person-to-person relationships. In his encyclical letter *Laudato Si'* ("On Care for Our Common Home"), Francis describes the transformative experience of encounter with creation. Using the language of ecological conversion, Francis invites people to experience themselves as part of nature, not outside of it. Reframing our relationship with the earth in this way inspires people to move beyond an instrumentalist relationship to creation, which values non-human life in so much as it is useful to people. Focusing on interior transformation, Francis calls out the harmful dispositions at the root of the ecological crisis: individualism, materialism, consumerism. While he expands CST beyond anthropocentrism, recognizing the climate as a common good and naming the intrinsic value of creation, Francis maintains the belief that the dignity of the human person is unique. Echoing the language of Jewish philosopher Martin Buber, Francis locates our dignity in our capacity for encounter: "Christian thought sees human beings as possessing a particular dignity above other creatures; it thus inculcates esteem for each person and respect for others. Our openness to others, each of whom is a 'thou' capable of knowing, loving and entering into dialogue, remains the source of our nobility as human persons" (*Laudato Si'* 119).

Encounter, in this context, expresses human dignity through our openness to know and love another person and our capacity for dialogue. Here, Francis underscores the theological assertion that, being created in the image and likeness of an inherently relational trinitarian God, the person realizes their dignity in and through relationship. Francis further highlights the social effects of encounter in his encyclical letter, *Fratelli Tutti* ("On Fraternity and Social Friendship"). In this text, he connects our capacity for genuine encounter to peace and solidarity across borders and divisions. Departing from the traditional rhetorical style of magisterial documents, Francis asks the reader to imaginatively enter the biblical story of the Good Samaritan (Luke 10:25-37) to reinforce the need to encounter and turn toward people who are suffering. He interprets the parable: "We cannot be indifferent to suffering; we cannot allow anyone to go through life as an outcast. Instead, we should feel indignant, challenged to emerge from our comfortable isolation and to be changed by our contact with human suffering. That is the meaning of dignity" (*Fratelli Tutti* 68). Suzanne Mulligan makes this dynamic concrete in *Dwelling with Dignity: Catholic Social Teaching and Homelessness*. Highlighting the "disruptive" quality of encounter in Francis's thought, she argues that meaningful connections with people experiencing homelessness is essential for transforming a culture that fails to see them and "legitimizes [their] exclusion."[4]

For Francis, this call toward an ever-expanding expression of solidarity is central to the mission of the church and demands of Christian discipleship. His is a church that goes forth toward the margins of society, that is itself evangelized by the poor in whom the good news of the gospel is profoundly real. Inspired by the theology of the people, an expression of liberation theology in Francis's home context of Argentina, the preferential option for the poor has not only social and ecclesial implications but can also be understood on the level of culture, where communities make meaning.[5]

Within this context, Francis calls for a culture of encounter marked by closeness, dialogue, and reverence for the person. He

---

[4] Suzanne Mulligan, *Dwelling with Dignity: Catholic Social Teaching and Homelessness* (Collegeville, MN: Liturgical Press, 2025), 36, 121.

[5] Scannone, "Pope Francis and the Theology of the People."

contrasts a culture of encounter from a culture of isolation and exclusion. Isolation, Francis argues, is perpetuated by forms of technology that give a false sense of connection but lack commitment and authenticity (*Fratelli Tutti* 43). Isolation is endemic to a world that has forgotten that we are one human family, evidenced in racism and xenophobia and reinforced by an economy of exclusion. Francis vehemently denounced an economy of exclusion, which perpetuates such extreme marginalization that people are left out, disregarded, and ultimately killed by oppressive social conditions. With attention to culture, he names the priorities and dispositions behind these oppressive structures. Echoing Pope John Paul II, Francis describes a "throw-away culture" that values having over being and reduces a person's worth to their usefulness within an exploitative economy (*Evangelii Gaudium* 52–53).

Francis also contrasted a culture of encounter from one of apathy or indifference. Guided by an idolatrous relationship to money, he argued, people have forgotten the sacred dignity of each person. This attitude makes people indifferent to the suffering of marginalized communities. Francis made this clear in one of his earliest public engagements when he traveled to Lampedusa, an island off the coast of Italy that has become a container for migrants seeking entry to Europe. Francis, modeling the solidarity he wanted to see from the church and the world,[6] challenged observers: "We are a society which has forgotten how to weep, how to experience compassion—'suffering with' others: the globalization of indifference has taken from us the ability to weep!"[7]

However, there is a group of people who have not forgotten how to weep for those who suffer injustice: leaders of popular movements, whom Francis lifted up as protagonists in creating a culture of encounter. Early in his papacy, Francis launched an annual World Meeting of Popular Movements. This gathering included people

---

[6] Meghan J. Clark, "Pope Francis and the Christological Dimensions of Solidarity in Catholic Social Teaching," *Theological Studies* 80, no. 1 (March 2019): 102–22.

[7] Pope Francis, homily, visit to Lampedusa, July 8, 2013.

who not only experienced the effects of economic marginalization but were also actively resisting it to secure land, work, and housing. While leaders of popular movements may or may not be community organizers in a formal sense, they enact social change by transforming power. Francis recognized the "special solidarity" they practice as "organized poor."[8] In his addresses to popular movements, Francis honored their agency and creativity, lifting them up as models of Christian discipleship and protagonists of hope.

Speaking to the 2015 World Meeting of Popular Movements, Francis uplifted their role in building a culture of encounter:

> This rootedness in the barrio, the land, the office, the labor union, this ability to see yourselves in the faces of others, this daily proximity to their share of troubles—because they exist and we all have them—and their little acts of heroism: this is what enables you to practice the commandment of love, not on the basis of ideas or concepts, but rather on the basis of genuine interpersonal encounter. We need to build up this culture of encounter. We do not love concepts or ideas; no one loves a concept or an idea. We love people . . . Commitment, true commitment, is born of the love of men and women, of children and the elderly, of peoples and communities . . . of names and faces which fill our hearts. From those seeds of hope patiently sown in the forgotten fringes of our planet, from those seedlings of a tenderness which struggles to grow amid the shadows of exclusion, great trees will spring up, great groves of hope to give oxygen to our world.

In this quote, we see how the practices of face-to-face organizing give concrete expression to the kind of encounter foundational to CST. Rooted in proximity to others in places where we live out our hopes or longings for change—in our work, homes, and neighborhoods—leaders of popular movements live out the commandment to love in concrete ways. Francis recognized the commitment that

---

[8] Pope Francis, "Address, Participants in the World Meeting of Popular Movements," October 28, 2014.

emerges out of relationships with others—not abstract ideas but "proximity to their share of troubles."[9] In his affirmation of popular movements, Francis lifted up a powerful practice of organizing: the one-to-one.

The One-to-One: People Change People

The relational meeting or one-to-one is a foundational practice in community organizing. Jeffrey Stout argues that some form of face-to-face relational meeting has been part of "each of the major democratic reform movements in US history" including the feminist movement, labor movement, and civil rights movement.[10] They are effective because people are more likely to remain committed to a project if they feel connected to others and experience themselves as important to the work.[11] Researchers have confirmed what organizers have experienced—that people are motivated by people, through stories, connection, and relationship. The one-to-one has proven particularly impactful in building commitment to common action.[12] Within the context of the one-to-one, people are invited to reflect on their story and what that story reveals to be most important to them. In the process of being heard and affirmed, they can begin to see how their struggles are not simply private matters but public concerns. In this way, the one-to-one allows us to begin to imagine possibilities for change.[13]

Observing a one-to-one from the outside, it would be difficult to distinguish it from a general face-to-face conversation. One

---

[9] Francis, "World Meeting of Popular Movements," 2015.
[10] Stout, *Blessed Are the Organized*, 148–49.
[11] Brian D. Christens, "Tips on Building a Broad Base of Engaged and Empowered Volunteers," Center for Nonprofits, University of Wisconsin–Madison (Fall 2011), https://sohe.wisc.edu/wordpress/wp-content/uploads/ChristensBuildingaBaseofEngagedEmpoweredVolunteers.pdf, cited in Whitman, *Stand Up!*
[12] Christens, "Tips on Building a Broad Base."
[13] Paul W. Speer and Hahrie Han, "Re-Engaging Social Relationships and Collective Dimensions of Organizing to Revive Democratic Practice," *Journal of Social and Political Psychology* 6, no. 2 (2018).

would see an exchange between two people, perhaps over coffee or on a walk, lasting around thirty to forty-five minutes. One might notice that one person was doing more active listening than the other—perhaps seventy percent listening, thirty percent speaking.[14] There would be eye contact and nonverbal communication that shows the other—"I am curious; I am listening; I see you." Yet, those who have participated in a one-to-one could tell you that there is something different about the exchange.

The person trained to conduct a one-to-one will know that it is strategic, organized, and purposeful.[15] They would have prepared for the meeting by (1) understanding their own story and rehearsing ways to communicate their story for impact, and (2) researching who has knowledge about a particular issue, a desire to improve their community, and influence in their community. The purpose of the one-to-one is both simple and relational—to get to know the person and what matters most to them—as well as targeted and specific—to enable the person to gain clarity about their motivation, self-interest, and desires for their community.[16]

The one-to-one is a starting point from which organizers build upon the relationship through subsequent meetings. It also allows organizers to gain a deeper understanding of what is most important to the community and to identify community leaders. The goal at the heart of this style of organizing is to help communities name the self-interests embedded in their stories, make connections across stories and, in doing so, build collective power. We will discuss the central role of storytelling and the ways organizers understand and engage power in subsequent chapters. Now that we have identified what the one-to-one is, we want to highlight what the one-to-one is not.

---

[14] Jesuits West Collaborative Organizing for Racial Equity (CORE) handout, developed by Annie Fox, "How to Do a 1:1."

[15] Jacobsen, *Doing Justice*, 86.

[16] Jacobsen, *Doing Justice*; Robert Linthicum, *Transforming Power: Biblical Strategies for Making a Difference in Your Community* (Downers Grove, IL: InterVarsity Press, 2003).

While the one-to-one is purposeful and planned, it is not driven by the agenda of the organizer. Jacobsen notes, "It is not a sales pitch. It is not a means of asking another person to do something. It is not an attempt to recruit another person to one's point of view."[17] The organizer asks open-ended questions that are designed to draw out someone's story and to elicit an articulation of their values, passions, and hopes for their communities.

How to conduct a one-to-one[18]

1. Start the conversation by introducing yourself, sharing why you initiated the conversation (e.g., "I am part of this group interested in this issue," "This person suggested I talk to you").

2. Share your story to highlight why you care about the issue. The story should illustrate why you care by recounting your personal experience. The goal is not to present an argument about the issue but to share about specific events and people in your life that have led you to care about the issue.

3. Get to know your partner by asking questions such as:

    How long have you been part of this community? What brought you here?

    What are your hopes for the community? What are your concerns?

    Have you ever tried to address these concerns? What happened?

4. Conclude the meeting with an invitation to attend a meeting or an action, or to connect you with another person.

---

[17] Jacobsen, *Doing Justice*, 86.
[18] Jesuits West CORE handout, by Fox.

An essential element of the one-to-one is the emotional connection it establishes. Stout, drawing upon neuroscience and philosophies of language, highlights the role of empathy in the face-to-face encounter. When an organizer listens with intention and empathy, they experience the emotional impact of a person's story in their body.[19] The experience of having another person mirror the emotional impact of your story can be revelatory, affirming, and deeply meaningful. Theologian Aaron Stauffer explains, "The relational meeting challenges people to give an account of their lives and to make meaning out of experiences of personal suffering, love, loss, regret, and grief and transform them to publicly actionable issues."[20]

So, on the one hand, we can identify practical skills that make the one-to-one successful. These skills include the ability to tell one's own story, which will be discussed in the next chapter. On the other hand, we have arrived at a deeper level of understanding what makes the one-to-one so meaningful: the way that an organizer shows up in the conversation. Saul Alinsky named the essential disposition of an organizer, "What makes an organizer organize? He is driven by a compulsive curiosity that knows no limits."[21] Most of us can recall when a conversation partner has listened to us with genuine curiosity and when it has been lacking. It is a qualitative difference with consequences to the meeting. Jacobsen notes, "If the one being interviewed senses boredom or judgment, he or she will keep the conversation superficial and will not reveal much of significance."[22]

How does one sustain such curiosity, openness, and empathy toward the other? What keeps organizers going in this work? Many organizers articulate a spirituality behind the practice of a one-to-one that gives meaning and ongoing renewal to their practice.

---

[19] Stout, *Blessed Are the Organized*, 153.
[20] Stauffer, "Relational Meeting," 169.
[21] Alinsky, *Rules for Radicals*, 72–80.
[22] Jacobsen, *Doing Justice*, 86.

One-to-One as a Spiritual Practice

For many organizers, the one-to-one is a sacred conversation. Several people we interviewed explicitly connected the one-to-one to their faith. Some see it as an opportunity to encounter God in the dignity of the human person. Some describe it as a way to live out their call to Christian discipleship. Through reflecting on the practice of the one-to-one, organizers shed light on the meaning of encounter that Pope Francis made central to his social vision, and they help us imagine possibilities for becoming a more synodal church.

Attentively listening to a person's unique story, acknowledging their hopes and struggles, is a way to recognize and honor their dignity. Jacobsen describes, "One-on-ones honor the image of God within another person. The expectation is that a great discovery is to be made in seeking to know any human being."[23] Affirming this insight, one organizer with whom we spoke described his motivation to organize as a calling to encounter "the sacredness of people," specifically as they are "trying to become authors of their own futures."[24]

Others echoed the insight that human dignity is expressed and encountered as people become protagonists of their story. The one-to-one allows organizers to witness this process and participate in it. One organizer, describing the one-to-one, said,

> The goal is not to manipulate but to understand the other. It builds a kind of relationship in which you understand their story, self-interest, hunger to be a public person. And you respect more deeply something because of understanding their story. You take the possibility to reflect back to the person, the call that you see in them in public ways.[25]

---

[23] Jacobsen, 87.
[24] Interview with Jacob, October 17, 2023.
[25] Interview with Peter, September 19, 2023.

Discussing the one-to-one in the context of Christian discipleship, Jacobsen suggests that the practice allows people to participate in the fundamental question Jesus asks his disciples "what are you looking for?" By listening to a person's story with this attentiveness, the organizer participates in drawing that person toward their deepest longings and to join others who share their concerns.[26]

Another organizer connected the encounter with God in the one-to-one as well as the calling to discipleship by drawing upon the biblical story of the road to Emmaus (Luke 24:13-35). In the story according to the Gospel of Luke, Jesus's disciples are walking together from Jerusalem to Emmaus in the aftermath of Jesus's execution and burial. As they are discussing the events that happened and grieving the loss of their friend, Jesus appears alongside them and begins listening and asking questions. His questions move them toward insights on their experience. Similarly, the organizer described God as a "third party" present in the one-to-one. God's presence in the conversation, he believes, "brings a sacred quality to them."[27]

As we reflect on the spiritual underpinnings of the one-to-one, we can better understand the centrality of encounter in CST. Approaching a person with genuine curiosity, openness, and attentiveness to their story is a way of honoring their dignity. Organizers describe the encounter with a person's dignity in their expression of subjectivity: becoming authors of their history, transforming their private experiences into public concerns through their story. One characteristic of the one-to-one is that it is a non-instrumentalist encounter with the person in that it is free from an agenda beyond coming to know them. This is what Francis, following Buber, described as the "I-Thou" relationship. Jacobsen describes, "And so also the one-on-one interview looks not so much for the What as

---

[26] Jacobsen, *Doing Justice*, 88.
[27] Interview with John, November 23, 2023.

for the Whom. We are not looking so much for information about the person as we are looking for the person."[28]

In subsequent chapters, we will describe more concretely how the practices of organizing embody the principles of human dignity, subsidiarity, and solidarity so as to advance the common good. For the remainder of this chapter, however, we want to continue to reflect on how the one-to-one creates the conditions of possibility for a different way of living together both as a society and as a church. Writing in the context of the Synod on Synodality, we observe concrete possibilities for relational encounter to transform the church.

One-to-One, Relational Encounters, and the Possibility of Change

As a spiritual practice that enables people to encounter the intrinsic dignity of another, the one-to-one is a success in and of itself. Moreover, it is a powerful tool for enacting social change. This book is full of stories from organizers recounting their "wins," big and small. A win might be a change of heart in a politician or a bishop. It might mean a sizeable turnout for a meeting or public action. A win might be experienced as a successful campaign or empowerment of a community that was previously disconnected from each other. In all cases, it is through building relational power that change happens. This section will focus on the power of relational encounter within the church, as seen in a particular way through the synodal process, which Pope Francis embraced as a source of renewal for the church.

Speaking to popular movements, Francis saw an opportunity to renew the church through the ways they are "thinking and acting in terms of community."[29] Popular movements, Francis affirmed, are proclaiming the gospel through their proximity and solidarity

---

[28] Jacobsen, *Doing Justice*, 91.
[29] Francis, "World Meeting of Popular Movements," 2014.

with those on the margins. He saw this as a way to renew and strengthen the church: "The Church cannot and must not remain aloof from this process in her proclamation of the Gospel . . . I am convinced that respectful cooperation with the popular movements can revitalize these efforts and strengthen processes of change."[30]

Francis made ecclesial reform a priority of his papacy, denouncing clericalism and formalism that stifles the church's ability to meet people where they are. Rejecting a self-referential church, Francis wanted a church that goes forward, one that meets people where they are, like a "field hospital."[31] Francis embraced synodality, an ancient ecclesial practice that involves gathering and discernment as a tool for reforming the church. Francis, in line with the ecclesiology of Vatican II, which emphasizes the church as the people of God and Body of Christ, embraced the participation of the laity as essential to the synodal process. After initiating general synods on the family (2015) and youth (2018), and a regional synod on the Amazon (2019), Francis launched a synod on synodality in 2021.

Francis summarized his vision for the church at the beginning of the synodal process. By fostering inclusive participation in the synodal process through dialogue and discernment among all the baptized, Francis saw the potential for a "different" church to emerge. Francis desired a church in which the synod is not episodic but a defining characteristic. Practicing synodality, Francis hoped, would allow the church to become "a listening church," and "a church of closeness."[32]

Writing about the theological underpinnings and concrete expressions of synodality, ecclesiologist Richard Gaillardetz argues,

---

[30] Francis, "World Meeting of Popular Movements," 2015.

[31] Antonio Spadaro, SJ, interview with Pope Francis, "A Big Heart Open to God," *America* (September 19, 2013).

[32] Pope Francis, "Address, for the Opening of the Synod," New Synod Hall, October 9, 2021.

"A synodal, 'listening church' requires structures and processes that can support meaningful ecclesial interaction marked by the free exchange of views and insights among all the Christian faithful."[33] One of the ways the synod leadership has promoted this transformation is by making the synodal process intentionally inclusive by instructing bishops to consult broadly with the faithful and to "be attentive to those at risk of being excluded."[34] Within this group, the Secretary General of the Synod identifies women, non-practicing Catholics, young people, and people with disabilities.

The insistence on inclusive participation is rooted in a theology that recognizes the Holy Spirit as the protagonist of the synod and the *sensus fidelium*, or sense of the faithful, as a source for discerning where the Spirit is leading us. Being attentive to the lived sense of faith among the baptized invites the Catholic Church to embrace subsidiarity as a guiding principle for ecclesial authority.[35] We will develop the theme of subsidiarity and power in a later chapter. Considering subsidiarity in the context of the one-to-one, we would like to point out the way person-to-person encounter is essential for the kind of discernment that Pope Francis embraced in his call to synodality.

The working documents to support the synod integrate the practice of "spiritual conversation" as a means to evoke meaningful and inclusive participation. In this context, a spiritual conversation differs from a one-to-one in that it is highly structured to promote active listening and open sharing in a facilitated group discussion. It is similar to the one-to-one in that it invites deep listening to the other, paying attention to "spiritual movements in oneself and in the other person during the conversation."[36] A spiritual conver-

---

[33] Richard Gaillardetz, "Synodality and the Francis Pontificate: A Fresh Reception of Vatican II," *Theological Studies* 84, no. 1 (March 2023): 44–60, at 48.

[34] Secretary General of the Synod of Bishops, "Official Handbook for Listening and Discernment in Local Churches: First Phase, October 2021–April 2022."

[35] Gaillardetz, "Synodality and the Francis Pontificate."

[36] Secretary General of the Synod of Bishops, "The Spiritual Conversation," 2021.

sation ideally creates a particular atmosphere of trust so that people can speak from their heart. Trust, rooted in relationships, built through encounter, enables people to take the kind of risks together that make change possible.

One organizer, Toni, captures the transformative potential of a deeply relational way of being church using the image of a shared meal: "I mean, that is like the original model of church, I guess . . . Organizing is all about relationships. And it's all about the transformation that happens when we're actually listening to one another and showing up and asking hard questions." For Toni, organizing helps the church remember what it is about,

> but there are ways in which our church, when we look at its beginnings, has shifted into a lot of kind of memorized rote prayer, and we've become kind of disconnected from the meaning of it all. And I feel like community organizing helps us to bridge that gap [between what is practice and the meaning of the practice].[37]

Toni echoes Lucia for whom organizing was the key to renewing her relationship with the church. She differentiates the church as an institution with a set of rituals and doctrines to a church as a people. Organizing, rooted in one-to-ones, builds up a people. As such it is a model and tool for building a synodal church.

Toward the end of the book, we will pick up this theme with more concrete connections between organizing practices and the synodal process. First, we will continue to describe the core practices of organizing, which all build upon the one-to-one. The next chapter offers a more granular understanding of the one-to-one by unpacking the practice of storytelling. Just as the one-to-one illuminates the power of encounter, the practice of telling one's story helps us understand the meaning of human dignity as a core principle of Catholic Social Thought.

---

[37] Interview with Toni, October 10, 2023.

Chapter TWO

Human Dignity and the Person as Protagonist

Teresa, an experienced organizer, describes what makes community organizing a distinctive way of promoting social justice: "In organizing, it's not just about the results, it's about how we got to the results." She articulates how organizers build confidence in people and help them find their own voice. Reinforcing the practice of one-to-one meetings, she believes that "it is not about convincing people to do anything . . . [referring to the one-to-one] I want to hear what you have to say about something. Most people in our world are never listened to."[1] The way that organizers build confidence, community, and relational power is an affirmation of human dignity.

Teresa offers a concrete story to illustrate her understanding of what makes organizing unique and what makes it effective. Her first campaign as an organizer involved working closely with airport workers. Teresa describes the challenges workers were facing during contract negotiations: "It was difficult for them to be heard [by management]. So we went to meetings with them, to stand with them, so they wouldn't feel alone in spaces where they felt

---

[1] Interview with Teresa, January 5, 2024.

intimidated."² Over time, she observed leaders emerge from the community who took public roles in the campaign for better wages. She recalled one woman who "was petrified" the first time she shared her story on camera. Only three years later, the same woman advocated for herself and her community before the city council. Now, she is an organizer for her union, standing with other workers. Reflecting on this story, Teresa said, "It was an amazing experience of [seeing] someone grow in her own belief in herself . . . [organizing] is not just about winning what they wanted, but also to grow in their own belief in themselves."³

This chapter will focus on the principle of human dignity, which is foundational in Catholic Social Thought and central to community organizing. Teresa describes human dignity as the principle of Catholic Social Teaching that inspires her the most "because so much of the work is about seeing the dignity of the people next to you, and usually what we are fighting for is some kind of dignity being brought back to our people."⁴ One of the ways dignity is recognized in the person and brought back to the community is through storytelling. As discussed in the previous chapter, the one-to-one revolves around sharing what matters most to a person through telling their story. Whether on a person-to-person level of a relational meeting or in front of a camera during a public campaign, sharing one's story is an essential element of organizing and concrete expression of human dignity.

What Does CST Say about Human Dignity?

Though rooted in Scripture and the foundational teachings of Christianity, the modern Catholic Social Tradition emerged in response to the reality of work and related social conditions brought about by the Industrial Revolution. In the first major social encyclical,

---

² Interview with Teresa, January 5, 2024.
³ Interview with Teresa, January 5, 2024.
⁴ Interview with Teresa, January 5, 2024.

Rerum Novarum ("Rights and Duties of Capital and Labor"), Pope Leo XIII denounces unsafe working conditions, child labor, and unjust wages and calls upon the state to protect the common good through labor regulations and a legal living wage. The pope's countercultural defense of the worker and their right to form unions, rest, and receive sufficient wages to support their family and have private property, still familiar calls of justice today, was guided by a particular view of the human person: "No man may with impunity outrage that human dignity which God Himself treats with great reverence. . ." (*Rerum Novarum* 40).

As the context of work and social issues that surround it have changed throughout history, the church's response has also developed.[5] What remains consistent is an unwavering belief in human dignity and insistence that working conditions, indeed all social conditions, honor and support this universal characteristic. The *Compendium of the Social Doctrine of the Church* summarizes it this way: "Men and women, in the concrete circumstances of history, represent the heart and soul of Catholic social thought. The whole of the Church's social doctrine, in fact, develops from the principle that affirms the inviolable dignity of the human person" (107). This section will highlight aspects of the church's teaching on human dignity that are particularly relevant to the context of community organizing. Related to the belief in the person as a protagonist, a concept embedded in Catholicism and community organizing, are the themes of conscience, human rights, subjectivity, agency, and relationality.

---

[5] For example, Pope Leo regarded women to be unfit to work outside of the home, a position no longer maintained in Catholic Social Teaching. He also maintained a preference for a hierarchically ordered society, which many contemporary thinkers reject on the basis of human rights. For an in-depth exploration on how Catholic Social Teaching has shifted in its embrace of historical and social analysis since early CST, see Donal Dorr, *Preferential Option for the Poor and the Earth: From Leo XIII to Pope Francis* (Maryknoll, NY: Orbis Books, 2016).

In ways that echo the call in community organizing to grow the agency of individuals and communities in transforming their situations, the *Compendium* describes the person as a protagonist:

> All of social life is an expression of its unmistakable protagonist: the human person. The Church has many times and in many ways been the authoritative advocate of this understanding, recognizing and affirming the centrality of the human person in every sector and expression of society. . . . The origin of social life is therefore found in the human person, and society cannot refuse to recognize its active and responsible subject; every expression of society must be directed towards the human person. (106)

By describing the person as a protagonist, this statement elevates the subjectivity, moral agency, and responsibility of the person as features of a person's dignity. This is not just a philosophical presupposition. In a Catholic context, claims about the dignity of human beings imply a particular theology. Catholic thought maintains since a person is created in the image and likeness of God then human dignity flows from the *imago dei*.

In modern Catholic theology, human dignity is considered to be intrinsic—inherent in each person—and universal because all people are created in God's image. Here we find the imperative to move beyond parameters of race, gender, immigration status, or religion to seek justice for all people. The intrinsic and universal dimensions of human dignity also help us understand it as something we own and not something we can earn or lose, empowering people to claim rights owed to them by virtue of their dignity and not according to other measures like merit or social status.

One of the ways people encounter and express this innate and sacred dignity is through exercising freedom and agency. In Catholic theology, human dignity is associated with conscience. Vatican II engendered this understanding with its embrace of a historically conscious approach to theology and ethics and openness to the modern world. *Gaudium et Spes* locates human dignity in our innate "call to communion with God" (19) and in our conscience, which they describe as the "most secret core" and "sanctuary" (16) of a person. In practical terms, this means that people must be free from coercion so they can respond to God in freedom.

Gaudium et Spes explicitly embraces universal human rights and "basic equality" as a regulatory principle for social life, which flows from the intrinsic dignity of each person (29). Here we see the influence of Pope John XXIII in a particular way. In his 1963 encyclical on peace, *Pacem in Terris*, Pope John argues for human rights on the basis of a universal order inscribed in human nature and discovered through conscience (4–7). Peace, for Pope John, flows from an observance of universal human rights that transcend context and opinion. He goes on to list specific rights, which, like the United Nations' Declaration, includes both personal liberties as well as economic, political, and cultural rights. Reinforcing the social nature of the person, Pope John puts forth a list of responsibilities that correspond to personal rights and build up a universal common good. Two things are helpful as we consider practical implications of this embrace of the modern human rights tradition. First, it offers a common language, specifically natural law argumentation, to defend human dignity beyond a particular religion or culture. This can be helpful when engaging in public action and when organizing in a multi-faith context. Second, the human rights tradition in Catholicism counters some tendencies within modern Western thought that promote individual rights and liberties above responsibilities to the common good.

Whereas Pope John relies heavily on a natural law framework that allows him to argue for universal human rights, more recent developments in CST demonstrate a greater appreciation for the role of personal experiences, relationships, and subjective dimensions that influence a person. Returning to the *Compendium*:

> Man exists as a unique and unrepeatable being, he exists as an "I" capable of self-understanding, self-possession and self-determination. The human person is an intelligent and con-

> scious being, capable of reflecting on himself and therefore of being aware of himself and his actions. However, it is not intellect, consciousness and freedom that define the person, rather it is the person who is the basis of the acts of intellect, consciousness and freedom. These acts can even be absent, for even without them man does not cease to be a person.
> The human person must always be understood in his unrepeatable and inviolable uniqueness. In fact, man exists above all as a subjective entity, as a center of consciousness and freedom, whose unique life experiences, comparable to those of no one else, underlie the inadmissibility of any attempt to reduce his status by forcing him into preconceived categories or power systems, whether ideological or otherwise. (131)

Here we see how contemporary CST protects against reductionist views of the human person and elevates subjectivity, conscience, and our capacity for relationship as expressions of human dignity. A reductionist view of the person might recognize their value solely or primarily in their capacity for reason or their productivity. Conversely, the Catholic view recognizes each person as a sacred mystery with a unique story and conscience that only they can access. This has practical implications in how Catholics approach social issues, such as work.

Pope John Paul II makes this view concrete in his development of the dignity of work and rights of workers. His teaching on work develops the idea of the person as a subject, whose creativity and capacity for relationship reflect the *imago dei*. He points out how these sacred qualities of the person can be obscured and exploited for profit or personal gain.

In his 1981 encyclical *Laborem Exercens* ("On Human Work"), John Paul defends the dignity of the worker, regardless of the type of work or output of their labor. Interpreting the book of Genesis, John Paul connects work to human subjectivity:

> Man has to subdue the earth and dominate it, because as the "image of God" he is a person, that is to say, a subjective being capable of acting in a planned and rational way, capable of

deciding about himself, and with a tendency to self-realization. As *a person, man is therefore the subject of work.* As a person he works, he performs various actions belonging to the work process; independently of their objective content, these actions must all serve to realize his humanity, to fulfill the calling to be a person that is his by reason of his very humanity. (6)

The objective dimensions of work include actions, products, profits. The ways these can be measured and evaluated are qualitatively different from the person doing the work. For this reason, Catholic teaching insists that the concern for the person be placed above concern for profit and that, more broadly, the "economy should serve the person, not the other way around."[6] There are countless ways people are exploited for profit and treated as objects within an unequal economic system. Centering the principle of human dignity and participation, as argued by Clemens Sedmak and Kelli Reagan Hickey in *Counting the Cost: Financial Decision-Making, Discipleship, and Christian Living*, can help individuals and groups align economic decisions with Catholic Social Teaching.[7]

Focusing on work is helpful here, not only because it provides an important context for organizing, but also because it illustrates two important dimensions of CST on human dignity. It recognizes that the universal, intrinsic, and sacred value of the person is constant, affirming the dignity of the person doing the work, regardless of the work performed, wages earned, or recognition gained. At the same time, it recognizes that the person can be caught up in structures that are unworthy of their dignity. Work can be demoralizing, alienating, and exploitative. People cannot lose their dignity but it might be obscured by unjust structures or dehuman-

---

[6] United States Catholic Bishops, "Economic Justice for All: Pastoral Letter on Catholic Social Teaching and the U.S. Economy" (1986) 13.

[7] Clemens Sedmak and Kelli Reagan Hickey, *Counting the Cost: Financial Decision-Making, Discipleship, and Christian Living* (Collegeville, MN: Liturgical Press, 2023).

izing conditions. So, transforming those structures is a way of calling out that dignity that cannot be taken away or given by another person.

As noted in the last chapter, Pope Francis strongly denounced an economic system that treats people as "consumer goods to be used and then discarded" (*Evangelii Gaudium* 53). Following previous popes, he advocated for society to be organized with the person at the center, as "protagonists of their own history" (*Evangelii Gaudium* 121). Now that we have an understanding of what it means in CST to describe the person as a protagonist, a subject of history not an object, we can turn to the practice of storytelling in organizing as a concrete manifestation of this principle.

Why Stories?

Through Teresa's organizing story, we observe the process of becoming a protagonist in the leader who emerged among the organized airport workers. The leader, initially hesitant to tell her story, discovered in it a way to generate collective power among the workers. Without speculating the details of this woman's motivation, organizers have observed the hesitancy to share one's struggles because of the tendency to assign personal blame to problems while minimizing factors beyond individual control. One strategy in organizing is to overcome self-blame through identifying the systems and structures that have been set up to benefit some at the expense of others. When we tell our story, as organizer Gordan Whitman points out, "we draw connections between our experiences that expose the social structures that shape our lives."[8] This realization allows a critical shift that organizers describe when private shame becomes public pain.

Another reason organizers rely on storytelling is that it helps build the kind of trust and commitment needed for collective action.

---

[8] Whitman, *Stand Up!*, 66.

Pointing to the community building power of storytelling, Whitman states, "When you're working to create social change, you want to think of yourself as an architect of human relationships. The best way to get people into relationships is to ask them to share their stories."[9] One of the ways storytelling is so effective in accelerating meaningful connections among people is how they cultivate empathy. Stout describes two goals embedded in a community meeting "two sorts of connections will begin to take shape: emotional connections among the individuals who are mirroring one another's concerns, but also thematic connections among the stories, a number of which now appear to be about something more than the particulars referred to explicitly in them."[10]

Both outcomes in Stout's account are important. Seeing the thematic connections between stories moves a community toward identifying shared interests. For example, in the case of the airport workers, they might start to hear from each other a shared struggle to survive on their wages. As they share their stories, they see an issue of public concern emerge. At the same time, the exchange of stories cultivates a sense of shared humanity. The issue of wages is not abstract but embedded in someone's experience of having to make difficult decisions between groceries or gas bills.

Because of their humanizing power, stories can help build a culture of dialogue. While issues are often sources of division, stories frequently speak to unifying dimensions of the human experience. Whitman points out, "You don't need to know whether you agree with someone to hear his or her story."[11] This is particularly important in the highly polarized context of the US Catholic Church. Within this context, it has become increasingly difficult to cultivate dialogue around issues like immigration, gender, cli-

---

[9] Whitman, 72.
[10] Stout, *Blessed Are the Organized*, 155.
[11] Whitman, *Stand Up!*, 73.

mate change, and abortion.[12] When we become entrenched in opposing positions, some of us stop listening to the other, some even stop seeing the other as a person with dignity. Stories are a way to assert one's dignity and cultivate trust through shared vulnerability.

Marshall Ganz, who organized with Cesar Chavez and the United Farm Workers, argues, "Stories are how we learn to make choices."[13] The ability to craft a public narrative is central to Ganz's approach to leadership and social change, which he teaches at Harvard's Kennedy School for Government and with the Leading Change Network. Ganz's approach to public narrative involves three related stories—the story of self, the story of us, and the story of now. These stories build upon each other in a way that moves a community toward action for social change. Ganz explains, "By learning how to tell a public narrative that bridges the self, us, and now, organizers enhance their own efficacy and create trust and solidarity within their campaign, equipping them to engage others far more effectively."[14]

---

[12] The Pew Research Forum, for example, found that Democrats and Republicans have moved further from the "ideological center" since the 1970s and Catholics are as similarly divided as other Americans. Drew Desilver, "The Polarization in Today's Congress Has Roots That Go Back Decades," Pew Research Center (March 10, 2022), https://www.pewresearch.org/short-reads/2022/03/10/the-polarization-in-todays-congress-has-roots-that-go-back-decades/. Michael Lipka and Gregory A. Smith, "Like Americans Overall, U.S. Catholics Are Sharply Divided by Party," Pew Research Center (January 24, 2019), https://www.pewresearch.org/short-reads/2019/01/24/like-americans-overall-u-s-catholics-are-sharply-divided-by-party/.

[13] Marshall Ganz, "What Is Public Narrative: Self, Us and Now" (Public Narrative Worksheet—Working Paper), 2009, https://leadingchangenetwork.org/resource_center/what-is-public-narrative-self-us-and-now-public-narrative-worksheet-working-paper/.

[14] Leading Change Network, Marshall Ganz, New Organizing Institute, Peter Gibbs, and Shea Sinnott, "Organizing: People, Power, Change," 2014, https://leadingchangenetwork.org/resource_center/the-organizers-handbook/.

The story of self should present one's personal history by highlighting key choices—moments of tension, pain, or overcoming struggle. As such, it surfaces what is most important to a person, perhaps giving insight into their personal calling or vocation. Whitman argues, "In the end, our story is an argument for what we think needs to happen in the world based on our experience."[15] The story of us should present defining moments in a community that reveal the values that guide and inspire a community. Ganz, who is the son of a rabbi, identifies the Passover story in the Hebrew Bible as an example of a "story of us" for the Jewish community.[16] Finally, the story of now should highlight the critical choices the community faces in the present moment. It should present the defining tension or struggle that calls a community to action.[17]

Telling one's story for impact is a teachable skill that can be honed through practice. Whitman stresses the importance of ongoing practice in not only telling one's story of self but also in understanding the most salient moments to highlight. Telling one's story is not about recounting all the details of one's life but focusing on critical moments. He points out that the best moments might not be the most dramatic. Rather, one should focus on turning points, experiences that compelled us to make choices that have shaped who we are.[18] Ganz reminds us that all stories have three parts: a protagonist, plot, and moral. The plot should revolve around moments of surprise, tension, a struggle, or something that requires a decision. These have the most emotional impact, Ganz argues, because "Those moments are the moments in which we are most fully human, because those are the moments in which we have the most choice."[19]

---

[15] Whitman, *Stand Up!*, 71.
[16] Marshall Ganz, "Why Stories Matter: The Art and Craft of Social Change," *Sojourners* (March 2009), https://www.sojo.net/magazine/2009/03/why-stories-matter.
[17] Leading Change Network et al., "Organizing: People, Power, Change."
[18] Whitman, *Stand Up!*, 70–71.
[19] Ganz, "Why Stories Matter."

Developing your story of self[20]

The goal of the story of self is to illustrate your deepest values and core motivations by identifying moments of decision through struggle. Some starting points for reflection include:

> What do you remember about your parents? What were the core stories of your family? What childhood memories do you most treasure?
>
> What challenges have you faced in life? What life lessons have you gained from living through these challenges?
>
> What jobs or projects have you been involved with that really matter to you?
>
> What stories—from your faith tradition, great books or movies—have inspired you? Why are they inspiring?

Recall painful and hopeful moments in your life: Who or what made a difference for you in these moments? What did you learn about yourself and the world?

Our story of self becomes richer and more impactful as we practice telling it and experience ourselves as heard and seen by another person. Identifying the ways we have exercised our freedom and responsibility, experiencing the ways in which we have been formed by a community, brings us in touch with our own subjectivity and dignity. In other words, it allows us to see ourselves as protagonists. As such, storytelling can be understood as a sacred practice of asserting and honoring human dignity. In the next section, we will offer an example from an experienced organizer sharing his story of self to illustrate not only the applied skills of storytelling but also as a sacred practice of human dignity.

---

[20] Adapted from Ganz, "What Is Public Narrative."

Storytelling as a Concrete and Sacred Practice of Human Dignity

Nicholas shared the story that brought him to organizing. As a gay man growing up in the Catholic Church, he described shame as a "demon" that haunted him. The shame he experienced was perpetuated by homophobic bullies at school. He had left the church when he was eighteen not only because he felt rejected as a gay man but also because he experienced a disconnect between the public image of the Catholic Church and the church his Latina grandmother believed in, one rooted in Catholic Social Teaching on the common good and human dignity.

He was first introduced to organizing by an Episcopal priest during a period in his life when he did not identify as Christian and did not know if he believed in God. He recalled an organizing training when, gathered in a church basement with a group of sixty Episcopalians, some of whom were ex-Catholics, he heard Christians share "stories of pain." These stories included experiences of pain from the church. Hearing these stories allowed him to name his own pain and claim his anger. He shared his story in the group and experienced, for the first time, "being held by a community." Reflecting on this transformative experience, he said, "I stopped directing my anger at myself" and "I felt my own dignity."[21] Gradually, his shame started melting away as he named his anger at the church and the bullies from his youth.

Nicholas provides an excellent example of an effective story of self, with a powerful protagonist, plot, and moral. He provides enough context to understand the emotional dynamics and existential gravity of his decision in the church basement. His story of pain—from being bullied and shamed in his own church—is powerful and relatable. As a protagonist of this story, he generates empathy that frees others to recognize sources of shame in their

---

[21] Presentation by Nicholas Hayes-Mota, Prophetic Communities Conference, University of San Francisco (February 2023).

own lives. He illustrates a deep moral truth through claiming his dignity in front of a community that held him; no power or authority on earth gets to revoke the sacred dignity of a person.

Whitman describes what Nicholas's story makes concrete: "When I tell my own story to another person, or to a thousand people, I assert my humanity. Indeed, this may be the action that is most in my control that gives me dignity."[22] Experiencing within themselves the assertion of dignity in the face of dehumanizing conditions, like homophobia or other forms of hate, organizers are keen to recognize this movement in others. In many ways, organizers are midwives of human dignity by fostering confidence and forming leaders in the community to become protagonists in their own story.

When asked what qualities or characteristics make an effective organizer, one interviewee responded, "if we care about growing and creating the conditions for others to cross that bridge from powerlessness to power, from an observer to protagonist, we have to create faith in others, to take the lead, and to accompany them in learning the art of public leadership . . . It's like people who love other people."[23] Similarly we heard other organizers describe a way of being in relationship with a community that affirmed their assets, strengths, and dreams. This stance can be understood in contrast to a deficit framework that focuses on the needs and problems of a community. Even people dedicated to serving a community might operate out of a deficit framework and, perhaps unintentionally, reinforce the imbalance of power that keeps the community in need of charity. An organizer's job is to form leaders to build power within their own communities, to harness the resources and assets of the community to foster meaningful change.

One organizer describes a shift toward recognizing the agency and strength of a community. She was organizing for immigration reform near the US-Mexico border. They were planning a public

---

[22] Whitman, *Stand Up!*, 65.
[23] Interview with Jacob, October 17, 2023.

action but, out of concern for the vulnerability of the community, she hesitated to ask too much of them. Yet, she discovered in working with the community most impacted by immigration policy, that they were the protagonists in the struggle. She reflects, "We have limited vision, and for me I struggle with seeing out of scarcity and worrying that other people might feel tired or not want to keep going. But when I pose the question to folks who are directly impacted, and are the ones that are at the center of these actions, their vision, and their energy, almost always without fail, it is bigger and more ambitious than mine."[24]

The organizer is not the creator of human dignity nor are they a passive observer. The organizer believes in the person, they recognize their dignity even when social conditions obscure or deny it. Like Teresa, the organizer knows each person has a unique story that wants to see them become the author of their destiny. In their unwavering belief in the person, organizers make concrete the Catholic teaching that human dignity is intrinsic and universal. Within this framework, no one can take a person's dignity away or give it back. But by listening to a person's story, witnessing to the assertion of their dignity, an organizer can help form protagonists for social transformation.

---

[24] Interview with Toni, October 10, 2023.

Chapter THREE

Solidarity and Power

Kevin has been a champion for social justice for as long as he can remember. In middle school, he was bullied for taking unpopular actions like refusing to stand for the pledge of allegiance as a protest to the US invasion of Iraq. While he had inspiring and supportive parents, it took him a while to find his people, a community that shared his values. He experienced a turning point in high school when he attended the Ignatian family teach-in for justice. The teach-in is an annual gathering of Jesuit high schools and universities to promote action for solidarity. This experience of Catholicism was liberating and revealed to Kevin the kind of church he believed in. He found his people in a church that shows up in the struggle for justice.

Now a member of a men's religious community, Kevin is particularly active in organizing for worker justice. He is convinced that the church needs to actively and visibly show up for people, especially those who are oppressed, marginalized, or exploited for their labor. Reflecting on this, Kevin shares a story of standing with workers on strike at a major automobile factory. One morning, he decided to bring coffee and donuts to the workers on the morning shift. He was met with surprise and someone asked "Why are you here?" Kevin replied, "because you are here, therefore, the church should be here."[1]

---

[1] Interview with Kevin, November 7, 2024.

"I am here because you are here"—this sentiment expresses solidarity, a core principle of Catholic Social Thought. Pope Francis, surprising the world with a TED Talk in 2017, reflected on solidarity: "How wonderful would it be if solidarity, this beautiful and, at times, inconvenient word, were not simply reduced to social work, and became, instead, the default attitude in political, economic, and scientific choices, as well as in the relationships among individuals, peoples and countries."[2] Francis recognized a "special solidarity" that exists among people organizing themselves from the margins. Speaking to the 2014 World Meeting of Popular Movements, Francis commended those gathered for practicing this: "Solidarity means much more than engaging in sporadic acts of generosity. It means thinking and acting in terms of community." In other words, solidarity, for Francis, is not just a feeling but a way of being in relationship with others. It is expressed in concrete choices and actions like showing up with coffee and donuts for workers on the picket line.

In this chapter, we will unpack the meaning of solidarity in Catholic Social Thought, identifying the theological roots and aspects of its historical development. We will explore the ways organizing gives expression to solidarity and invites a particular understanding of power. This will involve addressing often negative assumptions about power within popular and Christian sources. The chapter will conclude with voices of organizers who connect their faith to practices of solidarity. A number of people we interviewed describe Jesus as an organizer and they understand their own vocation to organize within a call to Christian discipleship. For many organizers, like Kevin, organizing is a concrete way that the church shows up in solidarity with those who struggle for justice.

---

[2] Pope Francis, "Why the Only Future Worth Building Includes Everyone," TED (April 2017), https://ed.ted.com/lessons/why-the-only-future-worth-building-includes-everyone-pope-francis.

What Does CST Say about Solidarity?

Solidarity, like human dignity, is a central theme in Catholic Social Thought. Like human dignity, it reflects a particular theological view of the human person and serves as a guiding principle for social life. In this sense, solidarity is both descriptive—asserting that people are fundamentally interdependent—and prescriptive—making a case for how we should structure social life so that everyone can flourish.[3] Both aspects of the principle make a case for community organizing. The fact of interdependence, or the descriptive aspect of solidarity, lays a foundation for the moral imperative to act in right relationship with others and build up just social structures.

While Pope Pius XII first evokes solidarity to describe the common origin of humanity,[4] Pope John XXIII developed the principle in his social encyclical *Mater et Magistra* ("Christianity and Social Progress"). These foundational writings are still relevant today as they acknowledge the need for vulnerable workers to build power together through solidarity. John XXIII builds upon Leo XIII to argue for the need for worker associations and adds the language of solidarity to describe their appropriateness and urgent necessity. Referring specifically to rural agricultural workers, Pope John describes solidarity as an attitude: "Rural workers should feel a sense of solidarity with one another." Worker solidarity is essential so that they can exercise a collective public voice; he notices, "The lone voice is not likely to command much of a hearing in times such as ours" (*Mater et Magistra* 146).

Pope John goes on to elaborate on the signs of the times, noting a growing complexity of social relationships in a more globalized

---

[3] For a theological and ethical analysis of solidarity in Catholic Social Thought, see Gerald J. Beyer, "The Meaning of Solidarity in Catholic Social Teaching," *Political Theology* 15, no. 1 (2014): 7–25, and Meghan J. Clark, "Anatomy of a Social Virtue: Solidarity and Corresponding Vices," *Political Theology* 15, no. 1 (2014): 26–39.

[4] Pius XII, *Summi Pontificatus* (1939) 35–41.

world. This complexity has only increased in the twenty-first century with the interdependence of markets and movement of people across borders, a source of fracture in many communities. John signals a shift toward a global Catholic vision in his call for international cooperation, coupled with a recognition that vast inequality is contrary to the solidarity of humanity. He writes, "The solidarity which binds all men together as members of a common family makes it impossible for wealthy nations to look with indifference upon the hunger, misery and poverty of other nations whose citizens are unable to enjoy even elementary human rights" (*Mater et Magistra* 157).

Pope Paul VI advanced John's ideas by advocating for integral human development, a concept that prioritizes holistic human flourishing over one-dimensional models of economic growth. Many organizers still embrace this countercultural perspective in defending the self-interests of particular communities against the economic interests of the dominant few. In his encyclical *Populorum Progressio* ("On the Development of Peoples") the pope advocates for solidarity between nations to address extreme poverty and instability. He recognizes that peace is built upon integral development, which includes economic, political, social, and cultural dimensions. While speaking on a global scale, the pope's insights have immediate and practical implications that are still relevant today. The call to solidarity involves the transformation of social structures to foster participation and inclusive flourishing of all people. In the words of Paul VI, "An ever more effective world solidarity should allow all peoples to become the artisans of their destiny" (*Populorum Progressio* 65).

By naming the connection between solidarity and human liberation from injustice, an insight fundamental to relational organizing, Pope Paul reflects important social and theological movements that occurred after Vatican II. Through inviting the church to read the signs of the times, Vatican II not only fostered a more humble openness to the modern world, it embraced a historically conscious approach to theology. This, combined with a renewed appreciation for Scripture as a gift for the whole church—lay and ordained—set the stage for the emergence of liberation theology. Much has been written about the impact of liberation theology on Catholic Social Teaching.[5] In this section, we will highlight the significance of liberation theology on Catholic understanding of solidarity as it invites a reimagining of power in Christian theology that we see actualized in community organizing.

Liberation theology emerged on multiple levels in the church of Latin America, influencing bishops' statements and the work of academic theologians such as Gustavo Gutiérrez from Peru. Yet, as Gutiérrez points out, the poor who encounter God in their struggle against oppression remain the source of liberation theology.[6] Inspired by Vatican II as well as literacy programs aimed to empower impoverished communities in South and Central America,[7] people began gathering in small groups for bible study and faith sharing. Within these *comunidades eclesiales de base*, Christian base communities, the faithful were encouraged to interpret Scripture through their experiences. For those experiencing oppressive poverty and political violence, the liberating message of the gospel offered hope and inspired solidarity in the church.

A regional synod of Latin American bishops (1971) expressed this insight in "Justice in the World":

> Listening to the cry of those who suffer violence and are oppressed by unjust systems and structures, and hearing the appeal of a world that by its perversity contradicts the plan of its Creator, we have shared our awareness of the Church's vocation to be present in the heart of the world by proclaiming the Good News to the poor, freedom to the oppressed, and joy to the afflicted.

---

[5] See, for example, Dorr, *Preferential Option for the Poor.*

[6] Gustavo Gutiérrez, *A Theology of Liberation: History, Politics, and Salvation*, rev. ed. (Maryknoll, NY: Orbis Books, 1988).

[7] Particularly influential in this regard is Paulo Freire, *Pedagogy of the Oppressed* (New York: Continuum, 1968).

By denouncing oppressive poverty as an affront to God's will, the bishops identify how sin is embedded in unjust structures, a key insight in liberation theology. Through structural analysis, liberation theology highlights how power functions to benefit some at the expense of others. Beyond that, liberation theology presents a God who shares in human suffering and actively labors to transform oppressive structures so that everyone may flourish. Within this theology, the good news that Christians proclaim is that God hears the cry of the poor and takes their side in the struggle for liberation. The preferential option for the poor is central to the mission of the church, as stated in "Justice in the World":

> Action on behalf of justice and participation in the transformation of the world fully appear to us as a constitutive dimension of the preaching of the Gospel, or, in other words, of the Church's mission for the redemption of the human race and its liberation from every oppressive situation.

The call to solidarity expressed in "Justice in the World" reinforces the work for social justice, including the work of community organizing, as an expression of the church's mission.

As in the case of human dignity, the church's teaching on solidarity reflects a particular theological anthropology. Being created in the image of God who is Trinity, the person's call to community reflects God's relational nature as Father, Son, and Holy Spirit. Understood this way, human interdependence is not accidental or something to be downplayed. As such, Catholic Social Teaching provides an antidote to individualism. Within contexts shaped by Western liberalism, which emphasize personal rights and freedoms over the experience and demands of interdependence, Catholic Social Thought is countercultural.[8] Individualism, which is per-

---

[8] Todd Whitmore, "Catholic Social Teaching: Starting with the Common Good," in Kathleen Maas Weigert and Alexia Kelley, eds., *Living the Catholic Social Tradition: Cases and Commentary* (Lanham, MD: Rowman & Littlefield, 2005), 59–85.

vasive in many contemporary contexts, creates barriers to realizing the common good but solidarity builds it up.

Pope John Paul II connects the common good and solidarity in an explicit way by describing solidarity as a virtue:

> It is above all a question of interdependence, sensed as a system determining relationships in the contemporary world, in its economic, cultural, political and religious elements, and accepted as a moral category. When interdependence becomes recognized in this way, the correlative response as a moral and social attitude, as a "virtue," is solidarity. This then is not a feeling of vague compassion or shallow distress at the misfortunes of so many people, both near and far. On the contrary, it is a firm and persevering determination to commit oneself to the common good; that is to say to the good of all and of each individual, because we are all really responsible for all. (*Sollicitudo Rei Socialis* 38)

In *Fratelli Tutti*, Pope Francis reinforces the understanding of solidarity as a virtue that orients us toward the common good (FT 114). Francis describes the unique value of love as a moral virtue that goes hand in hand with solidarity: "Our love for others, for who they *are*, moves us to seek the best for their lives. Only by cultivating this way of relating to one another will we make possible a social friendship that excludes no one and a fraternity that is open to all" (FT 94). This encyclical on social friendship presents a vision of a world beyond ideological divisions and extreme inequalities. To that end, Francis denounces globalized markets that focus on economic growth at the expense of human development (FT 21). He also laments xenophobic attitudes and policies that deny the rights of migrants (FT 37–41). Finally, he critiques digital communication that promotes "information without wisdom" and illusions of connection without community (FT 42–50). Francis argued for practices of solidarity across borders and differences, which are essential for building up a global common good.

By describing solidarity as a virtue connected to the common good, these popes emphasize the importance of concrete practices in actualizing human interdependence and building up structures to reinforce it. Furthermore, a virtue, as a habitual practice, forms one's character toward a worthy aim. For example, we develop the virtue of honesty by repeatedly telling the truth, not just feeling truthful or being honest once. Another quality of virtue, as developed by Aristotle, is that it represents a balanced and prudent way of acting. Back to the example of honesty, a virtuous person would tell the truth in a way that is discerning and reasonable. When we consider solidarity as a virtue, we should practice interdependence in a way that builds up the common good and allows people to exercise personal agency within the community. In this sense, solidarity in Catholic Social Thought rejects individualism as well as extreme collectivism that leaves no room for grassroots organizing and local solutions to social issues.[9]

In the next chapter, we explore how the principle of subsidiarity promotes practices of solidarity in a way that fosters inclusive participation and builds up the common good. In what follows, however, we will examine how community organizers practice solidarity in a way that invites a reimagining of power. Organizing works because it builds power through engaging relationships, thereby fostering connection and leaning into human interdependence.

Community Organizers on Power

Power tends to be a highly charged word, evoking a variety of emotions and experiences, some of which are negative. Many of us associate power with expressions of dominance, fear, or experiences of powerlessness. History is full of examples of people misusing power in ways that offend human dignity and betray solidarity. Colonization, slavery, and political tyranny are extreme examples of the abuse of power. Less insidious but still harmful

[9] Clark, "Anatomy of a Social Virtue," 26–39.

include the consolidation of power in the hands of the wealthy, or political or religious authorities. When we experience power unilaterally or consider power as an expression of dominance, the adage "power corrupts" seems an appropriate warning. Given this, one might be surprised when organizers frequently and without hesitation talk about building power, analyzing power, and accessing power. Jacobsen notices:

> Organizers tend to have a rather straightforward approach to power. They want power. They want the people with whom they work to have power. And they want to build power organizations. They see power as essentially neutral. It can be used in the service of justice or abused in the service of evil.[10]

Jacobsen notes how Christianity promotes ambivalence or trepidation around power, presenting a challenge for organizers working in congregational settings. There are biblical warnings about the misuse of power and many examples of power expressed through violence, empire, and idolatry. At the same time, as highlighted in liberation theology, Scripture reveals a God who exercises power through solidarity with the oppressed and leads them to freedom from slavery or from ostracization due to illness or social status to life in community. The gospels announce the reign of God as an inversion of power as it has been wielded over the poor and the marginalized. Scholars describe a "great reversal" exemplified in Jesus's Sermon on the Mount, where the rich and powerful will be brought down and the vulnerable poor will be empowered by God's reign.[11]

---

[10] Jacobsen, *Doing Justice*, 55.
[11] For example, see Allen Dale Verhey, *The Great Reversal: Ethics and the New Testament* (Grand Rapids, MI: Eerdmans, 1984). See also Hak Joon Lee, *God and Community Organizing: A Covenantal Approach* (Waco, TX: Baylor University Press, 2020).

Reinforcing this theology, Martin Luther King Jr. reminds us, "power at its best is love implementing the demands of justice."[12] When considered this way, power is an essential part of the church's mission to transform unjust structures, as expressed in "Justice in the World." Writing about organizing in a Christian context, Robert Linthicum echoes King, "But in order to accomplish change, we have to learn how to use power. And as Christians, we must learn to use power in a Christian manner—relationally, not unilaterally—because relational power is of the essence of the gospel."[13]

Edward Chambers, who led and shaped the Industrial Areas Foundation (IAF) after Saul Alinsky's death, describes relational power: "As you become more powerful, so do those in relationship with you. As they become more powerful, so do you. This is power understood as relational, as power with, not over."[14] Relational power, or "power-with" is built from the bottom up and sustained through commitment to relationships. Relational power is *real* power, enabling people to act together and influence people and policies that allow change to happen.

Organizers often explain that "power is the product of relationship," which suggests it is most effectively cultivated and exercised collectively. Organizer and Lutheran pastor Alexia Salvatierra argues that, "A perspective on power that emphasizes the choice and capacity of the individual indirectly supports the maintenance of an unjust distribution of power by obscuring broader dynamics."[15] She draws upon Latinx spirituality and experiences to argue that power is dynamic and fluid, individual and collective at the same

---

[12] Martin Luther King Jr., "Where Do We Go from Here?" (August 15, 1967), available through The Martin Luther King Jr. Research and Education Institute at Stanford University, https://kinginstitute.stanford.edu/where-do-we-go-here.

[13] Linthicum, *Transforming Power*, 20.

[14] Edward T. Chambers, *Roots for Radicals: Organizing for Power, Action, and Justice*, 2nd ed. (New York: Continuum, 2018), 17.

[15] Alexia Salvatierra, "Latinx Missiology and Faith-Rooted Organizing: Poder Espiritual y Justicia Social," *Journal of Religious Leadership* 18, no. 2 (2019): 85–106, at 97.

time. She draws upon the image of the Body of Christ in Corinthians to argue for collective power that requires the development and well-being of each individual part.[16]

We learn relational power and unlearn negative associations with power by practicing solidarity[17]—through one-to-ones, community meetings, research, and public action—these practices will be developed in more detail in the next chapter. For now, it is important to note the way solidarity inspires and expresses relational power. Organizers build power through relationships, activating solidarity by fostering practices of interdependence. Gordon Whitman observes in his book *Stand Up!* that solidarity is built around shared purpose. Reinforcing the foundational practices of organizing, he notes that shared purpose is discovered through one-to-ones and storytelling.

Building Power as a Spiritual Practice of Solidarity

This section will present the act of building power through solidarity as a spiritual practice, engaging the voices of organizers and Christian theology. In our conversations with organizers we observed a conviction that the exercise of solidarity, of building relational power, is an expression of Christian discipleship. We also heard from organizers a belief that action for solidarity and building up a community is integral to the mission of the Catholic Church. These christological and ecclesiological insights, which we explore in this section, invite an understanding and experience of relational power through solidarity.

Kelly does not consider herself to be an organizer, but she has been deeply involved and committed to organizing throughout her career in Catholic higher education. She regards organizing as a concrete expression of Catholic Social Thought, Christian discipleship, and the mission of the church. She explains how being

---

[16] Salvatierra, "Latinx Missiology," 96–99.
[17] Linthicum, *Transforming Power*, 181.

involved in organizing has shaped her understanding of power and her belief in Jesus. Far from being passive, she believes that Jesus was powerful and exercised that power in a particular way: "Most people, when they look at Christ, he is soft, nice. [He] gave people food and cured people. [They] don't see his whole life as a challenge to the status quo. He's got power—to gather people together, to confront people."[18]

Echoing Kelly, Jacob connects his work as an organizer to encountering Jesus as a powerful liberator of the oppressed. In our conversation, he lamented that Catholics are not taught about the historical Jesus. When we consider how Jesus, "a Palestinian Jew living under the Roman empire"[19] exercised a transformative ministry, we experience Christianity in a different way. Jesus emerged in a context marked by conflict. In this context, he took up the cause of the oppressed and powerless, confronting those who abused their political and religious authority. Having been formed by liberation theology, Jacob understands his work as an organizer as "creating the conditions for others to cross that bridge from powerlessness [to powerful]; observer to protagonist."[20]

Pope Francis reinforced a Christology that centers Jesus's radical solidarity with the poor and marginalized. In *Evangelii Gaudium*, Francis describes the preferential option for the poor as a theological category that helps us understand the incarnation. God not only became human but he "became poor" through the "yes" of a "lowly maiden from a small town on the fringes of a great empire" (*Evangelii Gaudium* 197). Jesus did not passively accept the power structures of the empire but challenged political and religious authorities who exercised power through exclusionary and oppressive norms and practices. Francis describes solidarity with the poor as a firm commitment to social change: "Solidarity must be lived as the decision to restore to the poor what belongs to them. These convictions and habits of solidarity, when they are put into

---

[18] Interview with Kelly, July 27, 2023.
[19] Interview with Jacob, October 17, 2023.
[20] Interview with Jacob, October 17, 2023.

practice, open the way to other structural transformations and make them possible" (*Evangelii Gaudium* 189).

Organizing in a Catholic context, Peter understands that part of his work involves "overturning institutions." When asked to reflect on power, he said, "Organizing (real organizing) is focused on building power to change institutional arrangements, causing power to shift through organizing people and money and, for Catholics, it is about transforming the people doing the organizing."[21] Connecting this to his faith, he argues that the biblical mandate to "set the captives free" is not just a metaphor but a call to make change: "We are talking about people who are captive to poverty, consumerism, racism—releasing real people—and being freed by Jesus in ourselves."[22] Here, Peter echoes Francis's insistence that solidarity with the poor and marginalized involves personal transformation as well as the transformation of unjust structures.

Some organizers understand Jesus's ministry and command to "go and do likewise" as a clear mandate to build up community through relational organizing. Rene points out that "Jesus does not just go into a town and then leave people behind; but rather [says] 'come and go with me.' We are supposed to be a people—we are meant to be doing this work together."[23] This idea of "becoming a people" is central to organizing as a concrete way solidarity is understood and expressed. When considered in the context of Christian ecclesiology, it offers insight into the nature and mission of the church.

Pope Francis writes about the call to be and become a people in *Fratelli Tutti*. He regards communal belonging as an essential aspect of personhood: "each of us is fully a person when we are part of a people" (FT 182). He also describes barriers to experiencing ourselves as part of a people including indifference, xenophobia, racism, and individualism. In the document, he rejects populist ideologies which exploit our longing to be a people to

---

[21] Interview with Peter, September 19, 2023.
[22] Interview with Peter, September 19, 2023.
[23] Interview with Rene, December 5, 2023.

gain or retain power over others. Differentiating his understanding from populism, he argues:

> A living and dynamic people, a people with a future, is one constantly open to a new synthesis through its ability to welcome differences. In this way, it does not deny its proper identity, but is open to being mobilized, challenged, broadened and enriched by others, and thus to further growth and development. (FT 160)

Francis develops his understanding of the dynamic bonds of a community in *Let Us Dream*. Written in conversation with community organizer and author, Austen Ivereigh, Pope Francis highlights several elements of organizing in becoming a people, including shared story, communal memory, assembly, and building community through shared struggle. Connecting the idea of being a people with solidarity, he writes: "At the beginning of the story of every people is a quest for dignity and freedom, a history of solidarity and struggle."[24]

Writing in the context of the coronavirus and economic and social hardships it engendered, Francis laments a loss of our sense of belonging to each other. We forget that we are "a people" when we fall into individualism, indifference, and forget our own dignity and the dignity of others. Recovering our sense of being a people involves remembering our shared humanity and shared story.

> The feeling of being part of a people can only be recovered in the same way as it was forged: in shared struggle and hardship. The people is always the fruit of a synthesis, of an encounter, of a fusion of disparate elements that generates a whole which is greater than its parts.[25]

---

[24] Pope Francis and Austen Ivereigh, *Let Us Dream: The Path to a Better Future* (New York: Simon & Schuster, 2020), 97.

[25] Francis, *Let Us Dream*, 39.

Organizers form a people when they engage in story sharing through one-to-ones. They build a people when they cultivate shared interest and shared purpose in a community. Finally, they build a people through activating relational power born out of shared story, shared struggle, and shared hopes. In doing so, they actualize solidarity and embody human interdependence embraced by Catholic Social Thought. The next chapter will describe specific organizing practices that organizers employ to access power.

Chapter FOUR

Subsidiarity and Creating Pathways to Collective Power

Rene, an organizer in the Bay Area, admits that the work of justice can be overwhelming. "I really didn't know how to do it," she says, reflecting on her early experiences of responding to entrenched social problems. "It's a big Jenga puzzle. I [was] so afraid to move the blocks around for fear that it would all collapse."[1]

Her secret for solving the justice puzzle? It all comes down to co-creating heaven on earth with God and others.

"Jesus came so we may have life and have it to the full," Rene says. "We are actively working with people to make that real. Community organizing moves our focus away from issues and moves it on to the people. Talk to me about housing or low income rent? That's complicated. But I can be for Mary, who is not able to work because she has two kids and they don't have a place to live. To drill down to *people*? I get that."[2]

Rene is in the midst of launching a broad-based community organization with the power to bring about the change people want, primarily by holding elected officials accountable to delivering the priorities of community members. She remembers a key

---

[1] Interview with Rene, December 5, 2023.
[2] Interview with Rene, December 5, 2023.

moment that transformed the people she was organizing from a group of "armchair shouters for justice" into a people "who actually put into action what they want to happen." An elementary school student was struck by a car and killed on his way to school. The school belonged to a parish, which was a member congregation of Rene's fledgling organization. Prior to the tragedy, school leaders had requested additional traffic signage but their calls were shuttled back and forth between the two municipalities the school straddled. "Basically," Rene recalls, "they had not been able to get anything done for their school on behalf of their people." But once they joined a collection of other faith communities in their area also looking to address public safety concerns, things started to change. The group organized an action and invited the vice mayor to attend. "Within two weeks there was a stop sign installed," Rene reports. "And now we have an ongoing relationship with the vice mayor to see how we can improve neighborhood safety."[3]

Rene credits her work with others to "build a church" out of this group of different faith communities. She does not necessarily mean this in a sacramental or doctrinal sense. Rather, through the group's capacity to do things for their community she experiences a shared commitment to full flourishing of God's people. For her, the difference between organizing as an approach to justice and more familiar expressions like charity or advocacy again comes down to co-creating. "We are helping to co-create. It's not a savior mentality. We're not trying to move people's hearts per se. We're dealing with peoples' lived experiences and lived realities and trying to make it better. So we're really concretely helping each person live their full life. We're not doing it for them. We are giving them the opportunity to have life to the fullest. So if that means lower rent, then we work with them to achieve lower rent so they can have life to the fullest."[4]

---

[3] Interview with Rene, December 5, 2023.
[4] Interview with Rene, December 5, 2023.

The goal of this chapter is to explore the dynamics of the principle of subsidiarity as connected to Rene's emphasis on justice as involving a commitment to co-creating flourishing with others. We will consider it as a method of drilling down on problems until we understand them as *people* issues that we solve together with people. This illuminates how community organizers are growing our understanding of subsidiarity as a set of spiritual practices around how we exercise power associated with co-creating heaven on earth.

What Does CST Say about Subsidiarity?

Saul Alinsky is credited with the central mantra of community organizing: don't do for people what they can do for themselves. While that sounds easy enough, how do we actually follow his advice? Given its roots in the word "help," subsidiarity shapes Catholic understanding of how we are called to respond to social problems, as individual Christian disciples and citizens and as members of communities seeking to flourish.

Pope Pius XI first articulated the principle of subsidiarity in the encyclical *Quadragesimo Anno* ("After Forty Years") in 1931. Through this teaching Pius took stock of the impact of *Rerum Novarum*. He was deeply concerned about the decline in the social fabric of society, namely the communal associations among people through which individuals exercised and received each other's gifts. He was also concerned about the effectiveness of emerging forms of democracy that separated the church and the state in responding to social problems. So he built on the principle of human dignity to articulate a vision of the social order in which Christian discipleship and political citizenship complement each other in a way that maximizes our autonomy and interdependence. He envisioned subsidiarity as the principle that protects the human person against two threats to their moral agency or freedom: excessive emphasis on community on the one hand, which can limit the ability of individuals to seek after their own flourishing, and heavy-handed governments on the other, which can squash the freedom of communities through which individuals are most likely to flourish. Perhaps Alinksy was echoing Pius's most succinct definition of subsidiarity:

> Just as it is gravely wrong to take from individuals what they can accomplish by their own initiative and industry and give it to the community, so also is it an injustice and at the same time a grave evil and disturbance of right order to assign to a greater or higher association what lesser and subordinate organizations can do. For every social activity ought of its very nature to furnish help to the members of the body social, and never destroy and absorb them. (*Quadragesimo Anno* 79)

From its initial focus on politics, the principle of subsidiarity evolved as a response to our increasingly globalized economy. In 1965, *Gaudium et Spes*, the iconic document of Vatican II that articulates the rationale and tools for the church's pivot toward embracing the joys and sufferings of the world, calls for subsidiarity in regulating economic relationships across nations so as to ensure the flourishing of all people (86c). Nearly thirty years later the US Catholic bishops name subsidiarity as a tool for fighting poverty, noting "it is wrong for a person or group to be excluded unfairly or to be unable to participate or contribute to the economy" ("Economic Justice for All" 15). In 1991, to mark the 100th anniversary document of *Rerum Novarum*, Pope John Paul II invokes subsidiarity in his implicit challenge of social welfare states and what we today might call the nonprofit industrial complex. John Paul envisions subsidiarity as a check against social programs that "deprive society of its responsibility," foster "bureaucratic ways of thinking," and lead to an "an enormous increase in spending." Subsidiarity by contrast helps us discover "a response which is not simply material but which is capable of perceiving the deeper human need." "In fact," John Paul goes on to say, "it would appear that needs are best understood and satisfied by people who are closest to them and who act as neighbors to those in need" (*Centesimus Annus* 48).

Pope Benedict XVI continues Pius's initial vision of a society that operationalizes subsidiarity when he names the church as one of many "social forces" that the state is called to acknowledge and support in order to accompany those on the margins (*Deus Caritas Est* 28b). Benedict also adds a spiritual dimension to subsidiarity, noting that it can awaken us to the divine in each other and orient us toward Jesus's gospel vision of union with God and neighbor. Subsidiarity "encourages men and women to enter freely into life-giving relationships with those to whom they are most closely connected and upon whom they most immediately depend, and demands of higher authorities respect for these relationships," Pope Benedict explains. "When those responsible for the public good attune themselves to the natural human desire for self-governance based on subsidiarity, they leave space for individual responsibility and initiative, but most importantly, they leave space for *love* . . ."[5]

During a general audience in the midst of the COVID-19 pandemic (September 23, 2020), Pope Francis encouraged us to use subsidiarity to build on the social bonds of compassion and care that many expressed and experienced during the global lockdown, in order to address and repair the fractures in our society that left so many vulnerable to COVID's deadly physical, economic, and social side effects. He contended, "in fact, there is no true solidarity without social participation, without the contribution of intermediary bodies: families, associations, cooperatives, small businesses, and other expressions of society. Everyone needs to contribute, everyone."

With that historical context in mind, we might understand subsidiarity as a political, moral, and ecclesial principle.

---

[5] Pope Benedict XVI, "Address to Pontifical Academy of Social Sciences," May 3, 2008, https://www.vatican.va/content/benedict-xvi/en/speeches/2008/may/documents/hf_ben-xvi_spe_20080503_social-sciences.html.

Subsidiarity as Political, Moral, and Ecclesial

Ultimately, if justice is about living in right relationship, then as a *political* principle subsidiarity maintains a balance between the power of governments and the collective power of people by safeguarding the peoples' abilities to participate in what Aristotle called the *polis*, or our public life held in common. It ensures that people are free to participate in communities that themselves are empowered to respond to social problems they face. In the same general audience, Pope Francis put it this way:

> Everyone needs to have the possibility of assuming their own responsibility in the healing processes of the society of which they are a part. When a project is launched that directly or indirectly touches certain social groups, these groups cannot be left out from participating . . . We cannot leave the people out of participation; their wisdom, the wisdom of the humbler groups, cannot be set aside.

Even so, subsidiarity also ensures that states or governments not leave their people unassisted if the problems they are attempting to address turn out to be too complicated or too big for any one group to tackle. Illustrating this point, Pope Francis highlighted the role of subsidiarity in responding to our climate crisis. Impactful change will require those in positions of inordinate power in our political and economic spheres, what some call the "grass tops," to support the grassroots movements of people in solving problems that transcend the boundaries of states or require cooperation among governments. So subsidiarity involves participation from bottom to top and top to bottom. "Let us keep in mind the principle of subsidiarity," Francis says in *Laudato Si'*, "which grants freedom to develop the capabilities present at every level of society, while also demanding a greater sense of responsibility for the common good from those who wield greater power" (196).

But subsidiarity is not only a political principle about how governments ought to act vis a vis their citizens. It is also a *moral* principle that animates the kinds of relationships we build with each other through political systems and procedures: relationships of consulting and listening, of believing and collaborating, of being transparent and accountable. In this way subsidiarity protects human dignity when we make the courageous decision to show up in the public square in order to collaborate with our neighbors about things that matter to us: our schools, our air, our criminal justice system; municipal government budgets; or the remapping of voting districts. It reminds us that everyone is called to participate in the ongoing project of building flourishing communities, that all have something to contribute.

As Rene explained at the outset of the chapter, subsidiarity reminds us that at the end of the day, we're not focused on social problems but on relating to *people*. Scholars of subsidiarity agree. Law professor Jeanne Buckeye contends that subsidiarity is ultimately about the hard work of human relationships: honesty, empathy, trust, forgiveness, hope. "Trust, psychological connectedness, and spiritual maturity—key virtues in a culture of subsidiarity—get stronger when tested, when failure and disappointment make it tempting to walk away, but people stay anyway."[6] To that end, Pope Francis called synodality a social virtue, since when we fully embrace its top to bottom and bottom to top "movement," subsidiarity can foster a much needed sense of unity in fractured and polarized societies.[7]

Finally, as we work together to become a more synodal church, where baptism calls all Christian disciples to participate in serving the mission of the church, the *ecclesial* aspects of subsidiarity are coming into focus. Many people long sidelined from formal discernment and decision-making processes in the Catholic Church—women, Indigenous peoples, young people, priests, and vowed women religious—are teaching us that subsidiarity is as much an

---

[6] Jeane Buckeye, "Exploring Subsidiarity: The Case of the Economy of Communion," *Journal of Religion and Society*, supplement 22 (2020): 66.

[7] Francis, General Audience, September 23, 2020.

ad intra principle of Catholic Social Teaching as it is an *ad extra* one. In other words, creating justice in the world will require us to practice subsidiarity through building just relationships *within* the church. Ecclesiologist Richard Gaillardetz highlights this growing edge of subsidiarity this way: "The primary responsibility for the realization of the individual Christian vocation and the fulfillment of the mission of local churches lies with those individuals and local churches themselves."[8] As a principle to be practiced within the church, subsidiarity also invites us to consider how we exercise authority across its different structures and roles. Gaillardetz contends that Pope Francis practiced subsidiarity through his effort to decentralize the Curia, or the bureaucracy of the church in the Vatican. Including women in leadership roles and insisting on synodal consultations increases the access of those closest to the pain of the world's problems to those in positions to leverage the church's resources in responding to them. In this way, Francis connected the principle of subsidiarity with the Catholic doctrine of the *sensus fidelium* or sense of the faithful: a belief that the Holy Spirit reveals truth in and through persons and communities of faith, and that this wisdom is its own source of church teaching.

Ultimately, the principle of subsidiarity guides us in working together within the church so that the faithful can better offer the church's resources to the collective task of solving the world's problems side by side with those most affected by them.

Subsidiarity as Building Paths to Power

In *Fratelli Tutti*, released during the first year of the COVID-19 pandemic, Pope Francis notes, "What [is] needed are new pathways of self-expression and participation in society" (FT 184). In a general audience, he linked subsidiarity to those new ways forward, stating that "this path of solidarity needs subsidiarity. . . . To emerge from [a] crisis means to change, and true change is done

---

[8] Gaillardetz, "Synodality and the Francis Pontificate," 58.

by everyone, all the persons that form a people. All the professions, all of them. And everything together, everyone in the community."[9]

Community organizers rely on subsidiarity to build pathways too—pathways to power, which we defined in our last chapter on solidarity as both a claim of human interdependence and a call to prioritize the community in our decisions and actions. Teresa, an economic and climate justice organizer, implicitly thinks of subsidiarity as the tool we use to build flourishing lives. "Jesus's whole life and ministry was literally walking into towns and communities and saying, 'I hear you, I see you, I believe in you and I want you to have the best in life,'" she says. "I think that's what most organizers are doing: I hear you. I see you. I believe in you. I want you to have the best in life. So how do we get there?"[10]

To figuratively walk with a community from where they are to where they long to be, community organizers use a set of practices with their people to forge pathways of participation, solidarity, and power. These tools increase a community's ability to effect meaningful change about what matters most to them in their own corner of the global church.

Participation

"Some have power and some don't," says Rene, in thinking about the root causes of social suffering. "We have to really keep in mind the call to participation; everyone has a right to participate in decisions that affect their lives."[11]

Organizers practice subsidiarity by building a variety of incremental pathways to participation.

The Listening Campaign

Just as a physician begins any exam by taking a close listen to the patient's heart, organizers usually begin any community initia-

---

[9] Francis, General Audience, September 23, 2020.
[10] Interview with Teresa, February 21, 2024.
[11] Interview with Rene, December 5, 2023.

tive by listening to the hopes and dreams, the laments and the visions of the people in it. Using the same ethos as the one-to-one, listening campaigns gather insights and wisdom from those on the ground in a community.

Through listening campaigns, organizers hear the stories of privately held shame in order to transform them into publicly shared pain that can motivate a collective response. Listening campaigns also provide opportunities to invite people to consider working with their neighbors toward a vision to be honed together. Listening campaigns can happen in the context of house meetings for small groups or community-wide town halls where neighbors share and receive each other's laments and dreams.

Leah, an organizer with the Faith in Action affiliate in Minnesota, recalls a listening campaign she helped facilitate in suburban parishes in Minneapolis-St. Paul, where pastors assumed they would have a hard time motivating their middle and upper-middle class congregants to get involved with community organizing because of their safe distance from much of the social suffering gripping lower income people in the state. Leah suspected that much of that suffering was closer than the pastors thought, and that "this demonic thing called shame" was keeping everyone separated from each other and from God.[12] So she convinced them to participate in a listening campaign in their congregations. An anonymous survey revealed that sixty percent of congregants were directly impacted by domestic violence and that a significant number were grappling with homes in foreclosure. All of a sudden, problems were not so hypothetical or distant.

"Listening campaigns change the nature of solidarity," Leah explains. "Part of a listening campaign's job is to organize encounters that add up to a community picture that creates more opportunity for people in leadership and those in the community to be connected with reality—*la realidad*—at a communal level. They create more solidarity, more grit, more determination for finding solutions."[13]

---

[12] Interview with Leah, November 11, 2024.
[13] Interview with Leah, November 11, 2024.

Listening campaigns are not only critical for community members. Organizers rely on them in order to be sure that they remain closely tethered to the self-interests and dreams of the people they are accompanying. "Subsidiarity is bottom up," explains John, a community organizer in Camden, New Jersey. "Decisions are made as close to the ground as possible. That's why we start with listening campaigns. We want to listen deeply and widely to how people are being impacted and by what. We build an organizing agenda based on that."[14]

Moving from Problem to Issue

When organizers attune themselves to what is happening in or to particular communities, subsidiarity helps them discover the difference between problems and issues. Problems are complex, multifaceted, and overwhelming. For example, where do we even start to solve problems like climate change or police-involved shootings or raising the minimum wage? But problems often manifest themselves as specific *issues* in our communities. Issues are tangible, decipherable, and fixable. The problem of climate change, for example, creates concrete issues such as higher rates of respiratory problems in communities in close proximity to the fossil fuel industry; the problem of police violence has particular issues like lack of community oversight committees in some jurisdictions; the problem of raising the minimum wage has particular issues like unjust food service contracts at universities or sports arenas.

Leah recalls that after discovering through their listening campaign the prevalence of domestic violence in faith communities across the state, congregations rolled up their sleeves to figure out what issues were contributing to that epidemic. Again, through listening to a variety of community members with a stake in finding a solution, they learned that most police departments were not using anti-domestic violence resources already allotted to

[14] Interview with John, November 11, 2024.

them. Now, the community had an issue: getting law enforcement to commit to using those resources.

John lifts up how a community he worked with wanted to address the problem of crime. A listening campaign that involved more than 500 one-to-ones revealed that many residents were worried about how vacant properties on their block seemed to attract all kinds of illegal behavior. Solving crime in Camden? That's a problem. Tackling vacant properties in particular neighborhoods? That's a specific issue connected to the problem of crime that the community could work together to address. The practices of subsidiarity—primarily listening and trusting in the wisdom of people closest to the pain created by big problems—help transform overwhelming problems into specific issues that people can tackle together.

Research Action Meetings

Another way that community organizing creates pathways for community members to "participate in decisions being made about their lives," as Rene puts it, is through meetings with a variety of people who can help a community better understand the various dimensions of the issue they want to solve and identify possible strategies for doing so.[15] These "research action meetings" have specific goals: build community members' sense of efficacy, or ability to effect change; establish or grow a relationship with experts or decision-makers connected to the issue; publicly signal the community's desire and growing capacity to address a particular issue; and gather information that will help the community identify the most impactful path forward in solving the issue. Ultimately, the group wants to leave the meeting with more relational power than they had walking in. Each member of the community who attends—usually no more than four or five—prepares in advance the agenda and the roles each will play: someone to open and close with prayer, a facilitator who helps keep the group focused on the agenda, team members prepared to ask targeted

---

[15] Interview with Rene, December 5, 2023.

questions, and a notetaker who shares back key takeaways and next steps.

Research action meetings position community members as essential assets for solving issues and as such grow their power to effect change. At a research action meeting with the staffer of an elected official to discuss the need for immigration reform, Toni recalls a community member who insisted on sharing video from his cell phone of the untenable living conditions along the border as a means of both credentialing the group and offering an insider perspective on the issue. "That was a poignant moment when everyone recognized this wasn't about words or numbers or theory, but this was about Roberto and his family and other families that are every day in danger when we refuse to take action," she says. "I don't like the wording of 'option for the poor' but I would say 'centering folks who are in the center of these issues.'"[16]

Mapping Assets

Ultimately, organizers use subsidiarity to tap into the primary asset on hand in local communities for solving the issues: the people in the community themselves. When we recognize the people closest to the pain are usually the people with ideas for how to eliminate it, we make an important shift in our perspective on that community—from one of need and deficiency to one of gifts and abundance.

The very process of mapping assets—inviting community members to identify their own gifts, resources, and relational connections and then to recognize the latent gifts and resources collectively held in the group—can awaken people to their individual and collective potential to effect the change they want to see. It's no longer a group of people with a set of needs waiting on others to meet those needs. Subsidiarity helps us harness the resources already available to a community when we shift from a paternalistic attitude of "doing for them" to a transformational attitude of "working with them." Asset mapping also helps community orga-

---

[16] Interview with Toni, October 10, 2023.

nizers avoid "Columbusing," a pitfall that good intending people with no real lived experience of the problem or issue at hand often fall into: proposing and then directing solutions that are new to *them* while ignorant that such solutions may already exist or have been tried or developed by the community.

Cutting an Issue

Once community organizations have broken down their problem into a potentially solvable issue and mapped the assets in their group and among their allies, they need to move from talk to action. They need to engage in the strategic work of determining the most impactful step they can take toward achieving their solution and setting the community up for its next win. "You can't just speak about problems," explains Leah from Minnesota. "It makes me mad when we take unprincipled shots in the dark. If something is important enough to do, it is important to be successful. You need to think of pathways to change. We want X from Y by Z or else A and B."[17]

Known as "the issue cut" or "cutting the issue," this step involves all of those involved in the campaign weighing the possible solutions and strategies for achieving them using a variety of criteria: does this solution advance the self-interests of the community? Is it feasible? Will it grow the community's relationship with decision-makers? Will it engage decision-makers or pressure those with the power to make the solution happen? Will it be sufficiently visible? Will it attract others to the campaign and to the organization? Can we integrate faith traditions into our messaging and witness? Do we have people close to the pain who are ready to lead us? Ultimately, will this collective effort grow the confidence and commitment of the community?

Those involved in Leah's domestic violence campaign decided the most effective way to cut the issue of underutilized resources in police departments was to do a broad systems audit of multiple

[17] Interview with Leah, November 11, 2024.

precincts, a step organizers knew would require buy-in from every level of government. This would then grow their power in every public attempt they undertook to gain it while also increasing collaboration across government agencies around the issue. Signing on to the domestic violence audit became a part of the mayoral campaign in Minneapolis, and sheriff races at the county level. "It wasn't coming up with answers as much as creating the political will for people to prioritize the issue," Leah explains of the rationale behind their decision to cut the issue this way. "When the audit happened, the impact was massive."[18]

Cutting an issue is an exercise in subsidiarity because it relies on the laments and visions, the insider knowledge and networks of relationships, and the courage of communities with the most at stake when it comes to solving an issue. It also requires a refusal to think with the logic of the status quo—"nothing will ever change" or "this problem is too big" or "let's just cancel those we don't agree with"—and to rely instead the collective imagination of the community to design and execute a creative strategy for getting one step closer to their desired solution. "When we discern something collectively, our power can multiply," says Leah.[19]

"It's not about whether or not we can do something," Teresa from Philadelphia explains, "but rather that we *have* to find a way to do something. When we tried to work for a living wage and people told us it was ridiculous, it was a matter of finding a way to do it because it is the right thing to do. It's about pushing people beyond what they already believe and already know."[20]

Starting Small and Local

Cutting an issue also requires humility on the part of organizers. Ultimately, the community needs to define what a win will look

---

[18] Interview with Leah, November 12, 2024.
[19] Interview with Leah, November 12, 2024.
[20] Interview with Teresa, February 21, 2024.

like for the issue they want to solve. Teresa has found this to be particularly true in her current work on climate justice campaigns in a city like Philadelphia, where the impact of a changing climate is different from those in rural or coastal areas, and where it can be difficult for urban citizens to see themselves and their concerns represented in environmental justice campaigns.

She recalls a campaign that involved a community drawing up an agreement with a housing developer looking to turn a former school into luxury apartments.

> When you think of all of the things the community could ask for—which was hard to arrive at—when people got comfortable enough to say what they really wanted [was] green space. A place to grow fruit, lawns for kids to run across. It took months for them to say what they really wanted. I watched this 60-year-old woman stand up and say to the owners of the building, "My community needs this" and demand that he see her. That was one of my proudest moments. This is what environmental justice in an urban setting looks like.[21]

As Rene helped us see at the outset of this chapter, by privileging those closest to social problems as the ones who need to be supported in solving those problems, subsidiarity encourages accountability to *people* experiencing various issues and not simply to the issues themselves. "Pius began his statement of the principle with an affirmation of the rights and capacity of human beings as justification for the importance of small communities," explains Buckeye. "For him, the reason that larger structures serve smaller was that smaller structures are closer to human persons and can therefore be better understood and influenced by individuals."[22] Organizers echo this: "Trust in the power of small," you'll often hear them say.

---

[21] Interview with Teresa, February 21, 2024.
[22] Buckeye, "Exploring Subsidiarity," 228.

Power

Frederick Douglass is credited with saying, "Power concedes nothing without a demand. It never did and it never will." Subsidiarity, therefore, is about making better decisions about our life in common by expanding access to the decision making processes and increasing the accountability of decision makers to those most impacted by our social problems. To that end, organizers rely on subsidiarity to determine where and how to build a community's efficacy through the application of pressure or creating social friction. "There is a theory of change in organizing," explains John from Camden. "What's your analysis of how power is operating in your region? Who's calling the shots? What's the big change you want to be able to deliver at a community level? And what kind of power do you need to bring that about?"[23]

Determining Targets

Once a community has completed their issue cut, they need to bring their proposed solution to the issue at hand to people in positions of power or potential agents of change to do something about it. And they need to do so in a way that will compel these potential change agents to decide if and how they will exercise their power on behalf of the community. As we will see in more detail in the next chapter, organizers ideally seek to convert these power brokers into conspirators with the community in achieving their desired solution, since doing so can increase the social trust and power of all involved to effect further change. Once again, the principle of subsidiarity plays a role here, as organizers identify these agents of change they need to engage at various levels of organizations or governments in order to achieve their proposed solution, often beginning with those closest to the community and the issue itself. Moreover, recognizing the central organizing principle that "power is the product of relationship," community or-

---

[23] Interview with John, November 12, 2024.

ganizing seeks to create and deepen relationships with those targets or change agents in order to discover shared self-interests that might motivate shared action. This is why you will often hear organizers say "no permanent enemies, no permanent friends, only permanent self-interests."

"Organizing is figuring out how decision-makers can walk with everybody in making their decisions," explains Leah. John agrees: "It's about figuring out [how a campaign] can move us into new political relationships with this city council person or this state agency, and then trying to make sense of what strategic thing we could do that helps us win now and positions us to win more later."[24]

Agitation

Organizing is a form of justice that seeks to build the power of people to evoke responses from decision-makers, and then to respond to those reactions in ways that continue to build the power of people and ideally grow relationships with decision-makers. To that end, it is ultimately a kind of holy pestering, a way of calling people into the power granted them at baptism to work with God in creating together conditions of flourishing for all of creation. Many people would prefer not to be interrupted by such a call.

John recalls a moment of agitation with a pastor he had been accompanying for a long time but who remained distrustful of organizing as a way of ministering to his congregation, which was eager to engage in social transformation work. John had made all kinds of compelling arguments for the parish to join the local organizing affiliate—to no avail. "I finally said to him, 'Father, I want to work with you and your people to build something powerful here.' He came back with money for the dues."[25] What made the difference? Agitating the leader of that faith community to imagine what might be possible if he were to commit to collaborating with

---

[24] Interview with John, November 12, 2024.
[25] Interview with John, November 21, 2023.

others around a shared vision of the kingdom of God for his community.

On this point, Teresa in Philadelphia likens Catholic organizers to the conscience of the church:

> It is very easy for us to pray for a change, it is very easy to stay safe and sheltered in my congregation with the people I like and call them brothers and sisters and say I care. It is another thing to walk out those doors and say in front of the world something that maybe is not popular—like, Catholic organizers are requiring you to show up as a full Catholic outside of Sunday service. I know that's an "ouchy" for a lot of folks.[26]

Susan Engh defines agitation as "provoking another to love and [do] good deeds—to the doing of justice based on one's best abilities or aspirations."[27] Agitation builds relational power by inviting individuals to act on their "lamentations and aspirations"[28] or to be accountable to more than just their private self-interests or those of elites. Agitation is an investment in our people—the people we're in relationship with in our community-organizing coalition, and those with whom we are trying to build more trust. By asking our people to reflect deeply on their self-interests and animating purpose for being part of the movement, we can encourage them to level up their commitment, perhaps through a leadership role or bringing a much needed gift to the table or being more public with commitment in some way.

Ultimately, agitation honors the essence of subsidiarity by leaving the decision to participate in exercising our individual and collective power, as well as the pathways to building power, in the hands of the people closest to the pain. Given organizers' own

---

[26] Interview with Teresa, February 21, 2024.

[27] Susan Engh, *Women's Work: The Transformational Power of Faith-Based Community Organizing* (Lanham, MD: Lexington Books, 2019), 28.

[28] Bradford E. Hinze, *Prophetic Obedience: Ecclesiology for a Dialogical Church* (Maryknoll, NY: Orbis Books, 2016), 151–63.

passion for social change, subsidiarity is an ongoing lesson. Toni, working on the US-Mexico border, says of organizing: "I think that's been a big learning for me as an organizer—not to make a decision for someone else what they can or can't do, but giving in, always making the invitation, and always posing the question and letting the person make that decision on their own."[29]

Subsidiarity as an Expression of Co-Responsibility for Our Shared Mission

When reflecting on one of her first introductions to community organizing, Kelly recalls the reaction of a parish priest to her inquiry about what the church was going to do about some social problem or another. He simply looked at her and said: "YOU are the church. Why are you asking me? YOU are the church." She recalls thinking at the time, "*I* am the church?" which quickly morphed into a courageous resolve that has animated a lifetime of organizing: "They can't throw me out, I am the church." Now some of Kelly's biggest hopes for the church rest in subsidiarity: "I want more listening and learning. I want us journeying together."[30]

As she reflects on how Jesus engaged people in the stories of the gospel, Rene, whose story opened this chapter on subsidiarity, offers a poignant insight to close it. She notes that Jesus didn't arrive in a town, drop some knowledge on people, and then move on. Rather, he said, "Come and go with me" as a way of continuing to be in relationship with people, to accompany them on an ongoing journey toward flourishing. "We're supposed to be a people," Rene concludes. "We are meant to be doing this work together."[31]

---

[29] Interview with Toni, October 10, 2023.
[30] Interview with Kelly, July 27, 2023.
[31] Interview with Rene, December 5, 2023.

Chapter FIVE

The Common Good and Becoming a People Who Go Public with Faith

When we asked John, a seasoned organizer from Camden, to tell us a story about his work that most stands out to him, he recalled a dramatic moment when 1,200 people successfully held one local public official accountable to the community's vision of flourishing. This particular community in Camden had been identified as a site for a municipal sewage treatment plant that would service the wider county. It was not the first time the residents of this district had been tapped to accommodate public services their neighbors in more affluent neighborhoods did not have the appetite for. County officials had already turned over prime riverfront acreage in the city for a county jail and a trash-to-steam plant, eliminating opportunities for green space and decreasing property values. Not only did folks in this particular area have to live with wafting odors of sewage and less tax revenue to support public services, but they also knew that other communities were closing their plants and returning land to green space as the new one in their community came online. The folks in the city of Camden believed they deserved to be compensated for serving the larger community in this way. So they developed a "host benefit program," which articulated their demands: eliminate the cost of sewage treatment by one hundred percent for negatively impacted residents.

"The campaign was being viewed [by city government] as a handout," John explains. "But we were making a justice argument. You've got to stop dumping on Camden. Everything that nobody wants comes to the city and we have to deal with it all to the benefit of others."[1]

In other words, the community was calling for reciprocity: we offer you something, you offer us something in return. They were also agitating for the common good—not simply the interests of some in local government, or a narrow swath of taxpayers, but for the good of everybody. And they were doing so in a very public way.

"Community organizing builds community and it moves community together," John says. "It elevates a parish community within a larger community, within the neighborhood in which it is situated. It says, 'We care about our community.' It provides a more prominent role for the faith community."

In this chapter we'll follow the story of that community in Camden in order to explore the principle of the common good, which both orientates us toward the value of life in community and motivates us to recognize, create, and protect those goods—material and immaterial, tangible and intangible, intrinsic and pragmatic—that make life in community possible. We'll identify ways in which community organizing relies on public actions to grow these aspects of the common good by insisting that faith, while deeply personal, is never private. Rather, faith is something we bring with us to an increasingly diverse and polarized public sphere where the conditions for life in community get hashed out. Community organizing gives us a way for our discipleship to animate our citizenship in the name of the full flourishing of all people.

What Does CST Say about the Common Good?

Like all of the principles of Catholic Social Teaching we have considered, a theological anthropology anchors the common good

---

[1] Interview with John, November 12, 2024.

in an understanding of the human person as constituted by God to be autonomous (free to make choices about the desires they have for their lives) and relational (interdependent on others in fulfilling those desires). Feminist ethicist Margaret Farley articulates theological anthropology this way: "Human dignity requires the freedom for self-determination that is best actualized in the context of relationships of being known *by*, belonging *to* and being responsible *for* others."[2] The common good orients us towards an approach to human flourishing that makes autonomy and relationality the standards we aim for both as individuals and as members of communities. The common good sets autonomy and relationality as benchmarks for human development toward which governments should strive.

At the heart of Catholic notions of flourishing is the fundamental claim that if we are made in the image and likeness of a God whose triune nature is characterized by relationships of mutuality and reciprocity, then we too become most fully ourselves through similar relationships with God, self, others, and the earth. The common good creates the circumstances through which we experience and benefit from the goods that come from being embedded in networks of relationship. Pope John XXIII is attributed with developing this principle in his 1961 social encyclical *Mater et Magistra*, where he states the aim of social, political, and economic activity is the creation of conditions that "favor the full development of human personality" and "social growth" that attend to the good of all and not only personal interests (65). Within a few short years, it became an orienting principle for a church seeking to send its pilgrim people out into the world as agents of the church's mission: the common good is "the sum total of social conditions which allow people, either as groups or as individuals, to reach their fulfillment more fully and more easily" (*Gaudium et Spes* 26).

---

[2] Margaret Farley, *Just Love: A Framework for Christian Sexual Ethics* (New York: Continuum, 2008), 152.

So what kinds of goods are part of that sum total of the conditions of social living that allow each of us to achieve our own fulfillment? Some of these goods are material: clean water, safe housing, a living wage, and transportation. Others are immaterial: public safety, education, wellness, access to political processes. The principle of the common good also invokes the "universal destination of goods," a moral teaching of the Catholic tradition that dates to the first Christian communities described in the Acts of the Apostles: "All who believed were together and had all things in common; they would sell their possessions and goods and distribute the proceeds to all, as any had need" (2:44-45). To that end, Pope Paul VI notes in his 1967 encyclical *Populorum Progressio*, "[T]he right to private property is not absolute and unconditional. No one may appropriate surplus goods solely for his own private use when others lack the bare necessities of life" (23). Pope Francis echoes this in his encyclical on environmental justice: "I would observe that the Christian tradition has never recognized the right to private property as absolute or inviolable, and has stressed the social purpose of all forms of private property" (*Laudato Si'* 93).

Although it is something we experience as individuals, the Catholic Social Tradition contends that achieving our own perfection is neither individualistic in its goal nor privatized in its method. Rather, it is a communal affair, something we can only achieve with others. *Gaudium et Spes* puts it this way:

> [W]e are today witnessing an extension of the role of the common good, which is the sum total of social conditions which allow people, either as groups or as individuals, to reach their fulfillment more fully and more easily. The resulting rights and obligations are consequently the concern of the entire human race. Every group must take into account the needs and legitimate aspirations of every other group, and even those of the human family as a whole. (26)

Ultimately, the greatest of the goods we hold in common is the possibility of life in community in the first place. David Hollenbach notes that common good reminds us of the intrinsic good of life in community: "One of the key elements in the common good of a community or society, therefore, is the good of being a community or society at all. This shared good is immanent within the relationships that bring this community or society into being."[3]

The common good in the Catholic Social Tradition, therefore, contends that we are most fully ourselves in the context of relationships that honor our individual uniqueness while simultaneously fostering a deep sense of being connected to and responsible for each other. In *Sollicitudo Rei Socialis* Pope John Paul II articulates that connection between the individual and the collective by making the common good the end goal of the virtue of solidarity. Solidarity, he says, "is a firm and persevering determination to commit oneself to the common good; that is to say to the good of all and of each individual, because we are all really responsible for all" (*Sollicitudo Rei Socialis* 38). The *Compendium* deepens this relationship between solidarity and the common good by noting,

> The commitment to this goal is translated into the positive contribution of seeing that nothing is lacking in the common cause and also of seeking points of possible agreement where attitudes of separation and fragmentation prevail. It translates into the willingness to give oneself for the good of one's neighbor, beyond any individual or particular interest. (194)

Ethicist Christopher Vogt contends this self-giving attention to others in Catholic approaches to the common good lends it a covenantal rather than contractual dimension.[4] Where contracts are transactional and legalistic, covenants are transformational and relational. They create deep social bonds that make it possible for us to be illuminated by others' visions of the good life and to

---

[3] David Hollenbach, *The Common Good and Christian Ethics* (New York: Cambridge University Press, 2002), 3.

[4] Christopher Vogt, "Fostering a Catholic Commitment to the Common Good: An Approach Rooted in Virtue Ethics," *Theological Studies* 68, no. 2 (May 2007): 394–417.

commit our unique gifts to working with them to realize those visions. In such collective pursuits, we all flourish. Pope Francis implicitly captures this covenantal dimension of the common good when he notes in *Fratelli Tutti*, "Each of us is fully a person when we are part of a people" (FT 182).

In short, the common good is a deeply relational affair.

The Common Good as a Common Project of Becoming a People

Despite all of our technological resources for connectivity, we face real challenges in building deep and broad networks of relationship, especially with people whose experiences and worldviews are different from our own. Perhaps that is why, in these unprecedented times of polarization and demonization in our politics and within our church, Pope Francis suggested that becoming a people might be the most impactful way we can work for justice. "The word 'people' has a deeper meaning that cannot be set forth in purely logical terms," he explains in *Fratelli Tutti*. "To be part of a people is to be part of a shared identity arising from social and cultural bonds. And that is not something automatic, but rather a slow, difficult process . . . of advancing towards a common project" (FT 158).

Community organizers engage in that slow, difficult, and deliberate work of building networks of relationship that make it possible for people to advance together toward common projects. Catholic ethicist Anna Rowlands refers to this as the "unitive" approach to the common good, whose primary goal is to heal the fissures and fractures in civil society—dynamics like gender and race, citizenship status and ideology, religion and zip code. In other words, the common good is primarily about identifying, defending and strengthening the relational bonds that connect us.[5] To that

---

[5] Anna Rowlands, "The Politics of the Common Good: Contemporary European Challenges and Opportunities," *Modern Believing* 60, no. 1 (January 2020): 37–51.

end, community organizing serves the common good by fostering cooperation, mutuality, and reciprocity within and among various communities that make up civil society, particularly when engaged in common projects.

Community organizing involves the slow and difficult process of becoming citizens. Luke Bretherton explains that citizenship involves "participation in a system for representing, communicating, and legitimating the relationship between the governed and government."[6] In many ways, this is precisely what the 1,200 faith-based community members from Camden did when they learned they would be processing the sewage for everybody else in the county. Once they had developed their plan for a host benefit agreement, they proposed it to the Camden city council, who told them such agreements were the purview of the state assembly. So they turned their focus on legislators in Trenton, the state capital, and finally identified one who would work with them to draft a bill that would include the host benefit agreement, but it would need to be passed by the assembly before they could go back to the Camden city council to begin the nitty gritty work of negotiating the actual discount rate they desired. "This is the big difference between charity and justice work," explains John. "There's a strong appeal with charity work. I know the time commitment. I know I will serve X amount of people and I will have the self-gratification of doing something that has immediate impact. With organizing, it's so stretched out. Solving one problem often creates another."[7] And yet, the arduous process of motivating the political will of city and state officials only bolstered the resolve of those involved in the campaign.

Bretherton notes that organizers remind us that citizenship involves developing a shared sense of the good life and shared sense of how to create it together, or what he calls a "shared political rationality." Organizing creates what he calls "a perspective

[6] Luke Bretherton, *Resurrecting Democracy: Faith, Citizenship, and the Politics of a Common Life* (New York: Cambridge University Press, 2015), 142.
[7] Interview with John, November 11, 2024.

of commonality" by "enabling participants to move from being 'groupies' with unreflective self-interests to citizens who are reflective about their self-interests and actively seeking mutual interests with others beyond their immediate identity or interest group."[8]

"It's part of what I love because it means that I get to show up as my whole self and sometimes I don't have to argue logic with you," explains Teresa, our organizer from Philadelphia. "It's not about whether or not we can do something but rather that we have to find a way to do something. When we tried to work for a living wage at the Philadelphia airport, people told us it was ridiculous. It was a matter of finding a way to do it because it is the right thing to do. It's about pushing people beyond what they already believe and already know."

Community organizing also involves the slow and difficult process of becoming citizens with a pluralistic sensibility. When people go public with their faith, they step out into social climates increasingly characterized by suspicion and mistrust. We are increasingly fearful people from diverse cultures, ethnicities, religions and expressions of religious disaffiliation, and racial and gendered identities. Trust in social institutions, including government and churches, is down. We are also confronted with communities fragmented by political and religious ideologies that fuel divide and conquer mentalities around issues such as immigration, climate change, gender, and health care. Increasingly, this fear, polarization, and fracture characterize faith traditions themselves.

These realities, which challenge even the notion of a "common good," necessitate that becoming a people requires an ethos of pluralism. The Pluralism Project at Harvard University explains that "pluralism is the process of creating a society through critical and self-critical encounters with one another, acknowledging, rather than hiding, our deepest differences."[9] Rather than exclude or isolate

---

[8] Bretherton, *Resurrecting Democracy*, 142.
[9] Harvard University, The Pluralism Project, "From Diversity to Pluralism," 2020, https://pluralism.org/from-diversity-to-pluralism.

those who are different, or force them to assimilate to the dominant framework, or seek a lowest common denominator in order to tolerate each other, pluralism encourages that we engage each other and participate together in the public square precisely through our differences. This is possible when we commit ourselves to learning about each other, get curious about what we hold in common and where our true differences lie, and make space at tables of public discourse—figurative and literal—for people to "come as you are, with all your differences and particularities, pledging only to the common civic demands of American citizenship."[10]

In truth, we can best discover the sum conditions for life in community when we seek them with people with diverse perspectives and experiences. We can more easily build those goods via broad coalitions of people with diverse gifts to lend. We can better defend those goods when connected to those who may not experience them as fully by virtue of some aspect of their identity.

"I was taught that God created biodiversity," explains Leah, the community organizer from Minneapolis. "I don't like Catholic chauvinism. Being deeply Catholic doesn't mean that my way is the best. Yes, it's my own culture and orientation but I believe our Creator can abundantly gift people in different ways and with different faiths. It's about trying to bring your best self and meet others in the world; and you don't need to do that by making [others] be like you. You've got to be a self among others. You've got to use a Ven diagram to find out where you and others overlap and figure out what to do when others aren't exactly the same."[11]

Pope Francis clearly called Catholics to embrace an ethos of pluralism. In *Fratelli Tutti*, he invokes the image of a "polyhedron," a multisided shape with no equidistant points, to help us navigate difference and disagreement: "Each of us can learn something from others," explains the former chemist. "No one is useless and no one is expendable. This also means finding ways to include

---

[10] Harvard Pluralism Project.
[11] Interview with Leah, November 12, 2024.

those on the peripheries of life. For they have another way of looking at things; they see aspects of reality that are invisible to the centers of power where weighty decisions are made" (FT 215).

Francis adds, "To see things in this way brings the joyful realization that no one people, culture or individual can achieve everything on its own: to attain fulfillment in life we need others. An awareness of our own limitations and incompleteness, far from being a threat, becomes the key to envisaging and pursuing a common project" (FT 150).

Ultimately, community organizing is becoming a people through public discipleship. An underlying reality here in becoming a people: faith is never simply private. It always has a public dimension.

Becoming a People as Public Witness

Becoming a people brings a public dimension to faith. Organizers spark the collective imagination for the common good by going public with faith, insisting that private interests cannot trump public ones and that visions, achieved through relationship, are essential to democracy. "If you want the kingdom of God to be true, instead of being mad about the sin in the world you have to be part of incarnating the Body of Christ in the world, being a disciple of Jesus who is loved at all costs," explains Leah. "I have stayed an organizer because I want the kingdom of God to be true, and for it to be true we need to participate in it together with others."[12]

At some point, the folks in that community in Camden tagged for a sewage treatment plant faced a choice. They could remain on the sidelines as vocally outraged but largely powerless individuals. Or, they could jump into the fray as an engaged collective with the potential to negotiate a different deal for their community. Their choice to roll up their sleeves helps us understand that the common

[12] Interview with Leah, November 12, 2024.

good is something that community organizers *do* and the messy public arena is the place where they do their work for the common good.

"I love Francis's vision as a field hospital or a MASH unit [that] mixes up with the world and doesn't hunker down behind the gates with fear of being contaminated, but has courage to go out and explore, to find where the hurt is in ourselves and others, and the systemic nature of where that comes from, and to address it together," remarks John. "Those are two different views of church—castle or field hospital."

Organizers' insistence that faith can motivate people out of the cheap seats and into the arena of public life challenges the growing sense of apathy and ennui about engaging in political life in general. Sociologist Richard Wood suggests that the "cultural shift toward disengagement" erodes a sense that it is even worth trying to seek goods together with others, leaving a political vacuum that populist ideologies like white Christian nationalism, with its narrow understanding of the good life and who is entitled to it, are only too ready to fill. People of faith going public with concrete suggestions for ways we might create the goods we need for life in community provide a viable alternative.[13] The "yes, we can" spirit is more than a rally cry but a way of doing politics by "manifesting the peoples' power to itself and to those in power."[14]

To be sure, this impulse to "go public" with faith or to link faith with citizenship cuts against the grain in contemporary American culture when it comes to religion and politics. Community organizing challenges the privatized and therapeutic strain in many religions, particularly Christianity, which insist that faith is simply a matter of private well-being or only concerned with hyper-individualized political issues. This posture tends to ignore the dimensions of faith traditions that challenge social suffering and

---

[13] Richard Wood, *Faith in Action: Religion, Race, and Democratic Organizing in America* (Chicago: University of Chicago Press, 2002), 264.

[14] Bretherton, *Resurrecting Democracy*, 157.

injustice. Liberation theologian and ethicist María Teresa Dávila suggests that the common good is best understood in terms of "orthopraxis" or rightly ordered action exercised in our public life together, as opposed to "orthodoxy" or right belief imposed on the public square. Orthodoxy privileges religious institutions and rules-based exercises of authority; orthopraxy privileges people animated by religious stories, values, and visions, and imbues authority with integrity. To break free of several decades of going public with right belief, primarily if not exclusively about the unborn, Dávila suggests US Catholics consider other important "goods of the Church" that the institution brings to a variety of places that shape our common life together: "outreach, public witness, family life, labor and work, politics, media, culture, the economy, and community organizing."[15]

Leah explains that after fifteen years of community organizing, she can list the potential challenges to the common good: "housing, jobs and access to contracts, affordable food, safety from domestic violence or gun violence or police violence, health care, the ability to take care of the people you love, a planet with clean air and water without lead in it."[16] It's just a matter of listening to communities to determine which is most urgent and then accompanying them in converting them from problems of private shame into issues of public pain that everyone is responsible for alleviating.

At the heart of Catholic approaches to the common good is an unapologetic claim that just like our social problems, faith is not a private experience, but one that sends us out into the world with our stories, our values, and our visions to work with other people of good will in achieving them. According to the *Compendium*, the responsibility for the common good belongs "to everyone and to each person, it is and remains 'common,' because it is indivisible

---

[15] María Teresa Dávila, "Building a Church of Liberation: Orthopraxis as the Public Shape of the Church's Common Good," *Journal of the Society of Christian Ethics* 42, no. 2 (2022): 265–72, at 269.

[16] Interview with Leah, November 12, 2024.

and because only together is it possible to attain it, increase it and safeguard its effectiveness" (164). Pope Francis notes that "no one can demand that religion should be relegated to the inner sanctum of personal life, without influence on societal and national life, without concern for the soundness of civil institutions, without a right to offer an opinion on events affecting society" (*Evangelii Gaudium* 183).

Peter, our veteran organizer from Minneapolis, implicitly highlights how Luke's portrayal of Jesus launching his ministry reveals the relationship between three tools that Christianity offers those who accept the invitation to go public with their faith—authority, agitation, and accountability. In going public with his plan to initiate the reign of God from the very center of his hometown, his own synagogue, Jesus invokes the moral authority of his religious tradition made plain by the prophet Isaiah. As a Jew like Isaiah, who was committed to keeping covenant with Yahweh, Jesus asserts his authority "to bring good news to the poor . . . to proclaim release to the captives and recovery of sight to the blind, to let the oppressed go free, to proclaim the year of the Lord's favor" (Luke 4:19). Like Isaiah, Jesus also agitates his listeners by reminding them of the primary responsibility of the covenant: to collaborate with Yahweh in stamping out oppression. Speaking from a synagogue in Galilee, at the edge of an occupied territory in the Roman Empire, many of his listeners likely had direct experience with social sufferings he named. Finally, Jesus holds himself as accountable to God and to his own people in living up to and out of this covenantal relationship by promising that the passage is "fulfilled in your hearing." This liberation is not something we're going to think and pray about; it is something that is going to happen, in fact has already begun in the very naming of it.

It's not hard to imagine the range of responses to Jesus's prophetic revelation in that moment: the contrast between what is and what could be, his unapologetic claim that change starts now, his confidence that transformation can happen. Certainly, it created pressure, tension, and conflict—all tools of community organizing.

"I think that one of my central tensions [as an organizer] is that it is crucial—if not outright essential—that we be involved in *worshiping* communities and that those worshiping communities are engaged in honest, powerful, truthful efforts to free the captives," explains Peter. "I think the line, 'this prophecy is fulfilled today in your hearing,' is about us and is about the expectation that what Jesus proclaims is now begun."[17]

The willingness to stand in that tension—between what is and what could be, between remaining on the sidelines or jumping into the fray, between platitudes and parrhesia or truth talking—and to collectively and publicly discern together how God might be calling us to act together, that lends community organizing its prophetic edge.

Community organizing relies on public actions to use that prophetic edge in building the common good.

Public Actions as Doing the Common Good

The community in Camden was tired of all of the punting with their host benefit agreement. After successful negotiations with city and state governments, the bill containing their state approved host benefit agreement had stalled in the state legislature. No one would bring it forward for a vote. The community decided it was time to take all of their private dealings with elected officials public. It was time to create access for the hundreds of people they had engaged in impacted neighborhoods to the decision-making process. It was time to bridge the gap between the community and the people making decisions that would impact it. It was time to leverage the people power they had built over the months of their campaign to stoke some political will to get the bill passed. It was time for a public action.

Organizers turned out more than 1,200 people they had engaged over the course of their campaign to a public meeting. They invited

[17] Interview with Peter, September 19, 2024.

the state assemblyman who had helped to initiate legislation to authorize the host benefit agreement in the state assembly in Trenton to attend. They ultimately asked him to take his commitment one step further by bringing the bill to the floor of the state assembly.

Community organizing creates the conditions for a common good: healthy democracy in which people can build shared visions and commitments across things that would otherwise divide us. It creates space and modes for public expression of faith in a pluralistic society. It builds tangible experiences of the relational goods at the heart of our common life together, which also make it possible to protect and increase material goods. And it forges relationships of accountability between people and decision-makers or powerbrokers. In other words, community organizers help us recognize that the common good is something we *do* together.

Public actions provide a key that people of good will can *do* the common good together. Simply put, public actions are public expressions of a community's power or its ability to achieve an intended outcome as a result of the relationships it has built. Public actions are a critical way that communities address the particular issue they have discerned as a result of research action meetings and issue cut exercises (see chapter 4). Usually, public actions aim to create generative tension: between the status quo and the moral vision of a community, between a community's goals and the priorities of its elected officials, between what is commonly known about an issue and what the community has come to know about it through their organizing. Here are some basic elements of a public action, which help us understand the common good as something we do.

Public and Plural Witness to Faith

Alinksy is famous for saying, "The tradition is the terrain."[18] By this he means that effective change movements necessarily unfold in the context of religious traditions because religions provide the tools for building what he called "a People's Organization":

[18] Alinsky, *Reveille for Radicals*, 153.

laments and aspirations that motivate us, values and stories that bind us together, leadership from within, rituals that make public witness possible. Religious traditions give organizers the authority to make bold public declarations about the common good that awaken our moral imaginations and the intellectual, emotional, and spiritual resources to struggle with people in achieving it.

"We finally won licenses for [undocumented] immigrants in Minnesota because the final public voice was Archbishop Flynn," recalls Peter from Minneapolis when reflecting about the impact of religious leaders joining their people in going public with their faith. "That was enormously powerful because it reflects a base, even with so many Catholics living with indifference about this [issue]. His presence raises questions: Why is the archbishop there? Where are *you* on this and why? What global indifference are you living?"

Theologian Brad Hinze calls faith traditions "the ballast" or the "spiritual center of gravity" of change movements.[19] Faith traditions keep us oriented to what matters and inspired to moving forward together. In their appeals to higher values or to "the more," faith-based organizers lean into religious traditions to lend their work a kind of moral authority that invites people to see their own stake in the big picture, to get into relationship with people trying to build the common good.

"When I walk into spaces with mayors and city counselors and directors of whatever, I start with prayer: you are a person that God loves," explains Teresa from Philadelphia:

> So I don't organize from a place of hate but from a place of love. I found you can't move someone who you hate—hate doesn't not move people, love does. I don't speak to you from a place of "you're a villain of the story" but "how do we make you the hero of the story?" People are more open to hear you when you come from that perspective.[20]

---

[19] Hinze, *Prophetic Obedience*, xxi.
[20] Interview with Teresa, February 21, 2024.

Leah in Minneapolis is unapologetic about what she calls the evangelizing dimension of organizing, since to her way of looking at it, community organizing is how we share "what we know to be true about God." In a statewide campaign in Minnesota to resist tax cuts for social welfare programs, community organizers developed a messaging campaign about shared beliefs in a God of abundance who provides more than enough resources to share with our neighbors. This helped reframe the responsibility of legislators: to grow revenue rather than simply reduce spending. "Getting to the big picture about who God is helps to clarify the choice that we have to make," Leah explains, "and to do so in basic human terms that don't get mired down in policies."[21]

Ritual

A distinct feature of faith-based community organizing is the plethora of images, stories, music, and symbols at the disposal of communities seeking to express their power in the public square and to grow commitments to the common good. Moreover, when done with pluralistic sensitivities, organizing can incorporate religious language into public messaging, images, and activities in a way that signals higher levels of comfort with expressing religion in a public square that is increasingly secular and intolerant.[22]

The Camden organizers opened their public action with a procession that visualized the campaign's main slogan: "You've got to stop dumping on Camden." One member of the community struggled up the aisle under the weight of an oversized garbage bag, symbolizing the negative impact of the trash-to-steam plant in their neighborhood. Another carried a giant sign with a picture of a jail. And finally, someone hauled up a toilet, representing the sewage treatment plant.

---

[21] Interview with Leah, November 12, 2024
[22] Wood and Fulton, *Shared Future*.

"That procession helped to communicate to folks in the room the injustice of one community being asked to take on so much for communities all around it. And that somehow, [doing so] was acceptable, was normal," recalls John. "It was also very empowering to city residents. It gave voice to their feelings of being less valued, less acceptable. It was powerful in the room to see people cheering the procession." John also notes how framing the issue through the lens of faith helped all involved appreciate "what justice demanded in this situation: that residents be compensated for providing this benefit to others in the county and the agreement be formalized in order to undo a pattern of environmental racism."[23]

In her embedded study of a Catholic congregation in the Roxbury neighborhood of Boston, ecclesiologist Susan Bigelow Reynolds witnessed the power of ritual to make visible a particular Catholic parish community's deep connection to its larger community. "By effecting embodied presence, ritual makes space for empathy, accompaniment and relationship where these may once have felt impossible," she explains. Ritual offers "an embodied itinerary for walking a common journey."[24] Ritual makes it possible for people who don't think the same way to be in deep relationship with each other nonetheless.

Public Agitation

A key component of public actions involves bringing the right people together around the right issue at the right time with the right proposal for what could happen next. You need the people you've listened to there. You need people who can offer moving testimonies to the impact of the issue there. You need community organizations aligned with your vision there. You need the people with the data there. You need people with the power to make

---

[23] Interview with John, November 12, 2024.
[24] Susan Bigelow Reynolds, *People Get Ready: Ritual, Solidarity and Lived Ecclesiology in Catholic Roxbury* (New York: Fordham University Press, 2023), 154.

decisions, or influence decision-makers, there. And depending on the hoped for outcomes, you may need the media there. Often, the hoped for outcomes involve convincing a decision maker to wield their power in a way that grows the power of the community.

After the state assemblyman had witnessed the "stop dumping on Camden" procession, heard testimonies from community members about the impact of being the recipients of the county's waste, and listened to a framing of the issue through the lens of faith, a Catholic lay leader presented him with a football. The number of the bill authorizing the host benefit agreement was emblazoned on it. Although he had been the initial elected official to do right by the community by bringing their request to the attention of the state assembly, he had allowed it to languish. As they handed him the ball in front of that assembly, they asked him to help get the bill "across the goal line" with the city council.

In short, they agitated him.

"Organizing has to present a threat or an opportunity to decision-makers," explains John. "I either partner with this organization in order to further my own power and advance in the public eye; or this could be a big impediment for me because if I don't work with these folks they are not only going to tell an internal story to the organization about how I didn't come through for them, but also through the media which amplifies the story much more broadly."[25]

This agitating dimension of public actions allow communities to speak truth to power: identifying contradictions or failed commitments, making visible the consequences of their actions, or presenting opportunities to build trust by serving the common good.[26] Agitation is a way of inviting those who are exercising power over people in particular situations into relational power instead.

Standing before those 1,200 citizens in Camden, with that football in his hand, the state assembly person agreed to bring their host benefit program before city council.

---

[25] Interview with John, November 11, 2024.
[26] Engh, *Women's Work*, 29.

"Was there a conversion for him or was it because he was on the spot?" Joe ponders. "It's hard to say. At least he recognized the political gain of moving the bill forward."

That political gain was a direct result of one community in Camden not being afraid of the tension that might arise in publicly insisting that a primary concern of government ought to be the full flourishing of all citizens rather than just the few with political connections. Organizers aren't afraid of conflict. In fact, they know conflict, friction, and tension are essential to the difficult work of transforming individuals and institutions to grow the common good.

Accountability via the Ask

The ask in a public action aims to build relational power by deepening relationships of accountability between the community and decision-makers who influence their daily lives, between leaders and those they lead. It seeks to build the power of decision-makers by reconnecting them to the power of the people they represent through deeper relationships of accountability: we'll all go further if we have each other's backs. Some approaches, like handing the football to the elected official in that public action in the city of Camden, seek to pin responsibility for getting something done on particular individuals. Others invite decision-makers into processes of evaluating possible solutions or discerning next steps. In either case, the community presents itself as a power player and tries to set up a win for the decision-maker as well as the issue they are trying to solve.

"In public actions you create a public moment for the community to tell public leaders what to prioritize and for public leaders to shine," says Leah.[27] In Camden, John notes, "we changed the equation by making it all about how powerful he is, and the

---

[27] Interview with Leah, November 11, 2024.

influence he has in the assembly, and we are looking to him to carry the legislation across the goal line."[28]

There are plenty of examples of Jesus publicly asking those in positions of power to rethink how they were using their power. This was a critical and prophetic element of his ministry of setting the captives free because he tangled with the forces of domination, which can be defined as "power minus accountability."[29] Ultimately, Jesus invited people into relationships of accountability or to live in a way that acknowledges and responds to others in a way that holds open the possibility for something new.

Stout suggests that community organizing is one of the most effective ways of creating accountability precisely because it disrupts domination. As we saw in chapter 3 on solidarity, organizing shifts power dynamics from "power over" to "power with." In other words, it generates relational power that is reciprocal, mutually beneficial, horizon expanding: I bring something to you and you receive it; you bring something to me and I receive it; and through these encounters, we achieve something new together.

Nicholas Hayes-Mota, a theologian and organizer, suggests that anchoring accountability in relational power increases transparency, responsibility, and responsiveness in internal and external relationships.[30] Internally, members of faith-based community organizing groups and movements exercise the virtue of accountability by prioritizing relational bonds of trust and mutual interdependence—relationships are more important than final outcomes. Also, orienting efforts around shared self-interests generates a stick-to-itiveness that keeps people in relationship with each other, particularly when the going gets rough. Internal ac-

---

[28] Interview with John, November 12, 2024.
[29] Stout, *Blessed Are the Organized*, 63.
[30] Nicholas Hayes-Mota, "Partners in Forming the People: Jacques Maritain, Saul Alinksy, and the Project of Personalist Democracy," *Journal of Moral Theology* 13, no. 1 (2024): 121–45.

countability lends the movement credibility and authority among the people with whom it works.

"Community organizing gives the church a way to be authentic to itself," explains Kevin about the relationship between accountability and credibility:

> My fear with the history of evangelization is that [it involved an] "I bring something to you, I have something and you need something" [approach]. More authentic to Christ is that "I bring something to you and you bring something to me and together we are church." "I give you something" is a great way to burn out, to end up empty.[31]

Organizers build on the deep trust among their people to bring external actors into accountable relationships with communities. Hayes-Mota notes that when power brokers and power dealers recognize a community's "ability to act effectively in concert" in ways that can either benefit or hurt them, they are more likely to collaborate with that community.[32] In this way, Hayes-Mota understands public actions as an "opportunity to create a new relationship of mutual accountability" between organization and power holders. This echoes Jesus's own prophetism in launching his public ministry: it calls people back into relationship with each other, especially religious or political elites. Hayes-Mota also notes that calling back into relationship was at the heart of Francis's understanding of what it means to be a people; it is what unleashes the protagonism or the agency of a people. The familiar "no permanent enemies" mantra in organizing "holds out the possibility of eventual transformation of both one's opponents—even the ones filled with enmity—and one's relationship to them."[33]

---

[31] Interview with Kevin, November 2, 2023.
[32] Hayes-Mota, "Partners in Forming the People," 123.
[33] Hayes-Mota, 123.

Conclusion

Alinsky once pondered, "Can there be a more fundamental, democratic program than a democratically minded and participating people? Can [humanity] envisage a more sublime program on earth than the people having faith in their fellow [humans] and themselves? A program of cooperation instead of competition?"[34] It's likely that the community in Camden agrees. In the end, Camden's city council agreed to a fifty percent cut in the sewage treatment bill for residents and businesses negatively impacted by the plant, a savings of $3.1 million a year and $90 million over the next thirty years. They had no sooner achieved that significant win when they were faced with a new attempt to "dump on Camden": they were targeted as a depository for huge piles of coal dust. But, having bolstered the common good, most notably their relationships with each other and their elected officials, through their participation in the political process around the sewage treatment plant, they were ready for the next opportunity to experience the common good in their struggle to protect it. They channeled their collective power from that win right into their next campaign.

---

[34] Alinsky, *Reveille for Radicals*, 197.

Conclusion

Synodality and the Future of Catholic Community Organizing

In *Let Us Dream*, the book Pope Francis wrote during the COVID-19 pandemic, he agitates those of us compelled by and committed to the church's social mission: "The church walks as part of the people, serving it, not trying to organize it in a paternalistic fashion because a people organizes itself."[1]

Throughout this book, we have contended that community organizing provides a way for the church to walk as part of the people and that the principles of Catholic Social Teaching provide the tools for the people of God to organize ourselves. In the first chapter, we demonstrated how encounters with other people's laments and dreams for their communities and our world, particularly through fundamental organizing practice of one-to-ones, helps us discover and commit to a central truth about social change: people change people. In chapter 2, we illustrated how prioritizing stories not only helps us to experience the principles of human dignity more fully, but also how stories catalyze change movements by transforming private shame that is too often dismissed into public pain for which we are all responsible. Throughout chapter 3 we reclaimed the concept of power, in this case power within and power with, by linking it with community organizers' understanding of solidarity: the ongoing spiritual process of converting from isolated individuals or

---

[1] Pope Francis, *Let Us Dream*, 106.

even tribal groups into a people with a deep sense of mutual belonging. In chapter 4, we considered the strategic aspects of community organizing—listening campaigns, research action meetings, asset mapping, and cutting an issue—as embodiments of the principle of subsidiarity through which individuals and groups exercise their protagonism in co-creating the change they wish to see in their communities. And finally, in chapter 5 we illustrated the ways in which community organizers go public with faith, primarily through public actions, in order to create a common good that is pluralistic and participatory.

In short, we have learned from organizers themselves that Catholic Social Teaching is a way that a people organizes itself when its principles get integrated into the theory of social change that animates broad-based interfaith community organizing: determine the big change you want to make with your community, figure out how power is at work in your community and who is calling the shots, and build the power within your community that you will need to bring that change about.

Synodality: The Growing Edge of Community Organizing and CST

In *Let Us Dream*, Pope Francis also lays out his roadmap for the future of the church, a path that he hopes people of good will walk together in this new epoch: synodality. He identifies key ingredients of this ancient practice of the church that will help us "meet each other with respect and trust, to believe in our shared unity, and to receive the new thing that the Spirit wishes to reveal to us" (93). First, we need "a respectful, mutual listening, free of ideology and predetermined agendas" (93); second, we need to hold space for what he calls "overflow" or the creative tension that arises when we engage difference or disagreements with humility in order to discover new horizons beyond existing options (80); and third, we need to be willing to engage in an ongoing personal and collective conversion process that requires patience above all. "Discerning in the midst of conflict," he wisely notes, "requires us sometimes to pitch camp together, waiting for the skies to clear" (94).

In the preceding chapters we have referenced the relationship between community organizing and Pope Francis's big gamble: that in becoming a church characterized by encounter and sharing our stories, of listening to each other and the Holy Spirit, and of communally discerning the steps we can take together to live out the gospel we will increase our effectiveness in serving the church's mission. In fact, synodality was Francis's signature contribution to Catholic Social Teaching given his insistence that this inherently relational and participatory way of being church together can be the church's contribution to a broken and suffering world. "We cannot remain inert before the questions raised by the women and men of today, before the challenges of our time, the urgency of evangelization and the many wounds that afflict humanity," Francis said in his homily to close the global Synod on Communion, Participation, and Mission. "Sisters and brothers, we cannot afford to sit back."[2]

Throughout the three-year Synod on Communion, Participation, and Mission (2021–2024), hundreds of thousands of Catholics stepped up and accepted the pope's invitation to walk the synodal path. Many witnessed—if not experienced directly—the invigorating dimensions of this ancient practice of discerning our life together as church. This included invitations to tell our stories of journeying with the church and with the same amount of time as church leaders, guidelines for actively listening for the wisdom in others' experiences, opportunities for candid dialogue with leaders about our laments and dreams, unexpected moments of courage to enter into rather than sidestep conflicts and tensions, chances to discover and even test drive relational ties that make risking new ideas possible. These are the fundamentals of community organizing.

---

[2] Francis, homily, Conclusion of Ordinary Assembly of Bishops, October 27, 2024.

For example, "conversations in the Spirit," the fundamental tool of synodality that allows participants to encounter each other in facilitated dialogues that ensure equality of voice and moments of silent reflection, are the ecclesial equivalent to one-to-ones given their effectiveness in affirming peoples' lived experience and calling them into community. This spiritual practice is the marker of a church that seeks to be synodal.

Or consider the invitation in synodality to speak from one's story and to listen for the Holy Spirit in the stories of others. This echoes organizers' confidence in storytelling as a way to honor the inherent dignity of all people by acknowledging the wisdom in their stories, the unique agency of storytellers, and the power of stories to transform people and situations. Organizers would agree with synod delegates' assessment that "[l]istening is a fundamental element of the path to healing, repentance, justice and reconciliation."[3] Synodality also reflects the orientation of community organizers—to be learners and not simply teachers, since in shared stories, especially offered by those on the margins we find the signposts for how we may move forward together, particularly through situations of tension and conflict. "The willingness to listen to all, especially those who are poor, stands in stark contrast to a world in which the concentration of power tends to disregard those who are poor, the marginalised, minorities and the earth," acknowledged synod delegates ("For a Synodal Church" 48).

Participants noted the latent potential of synodality for the common good, particularly the way we might build relationships between those at the center of power and those on the margins of society through spiritual practices of listening and communal discernment. "The synodal way of living relationships [is] a form of testimony offered to society," said synod delegates. It is a response to "the growing isolation of people and to cultural individ-

---

[3] XVI Ordinary General Assembly of the Synod of Bishops, second session, "For a Synodal Church: Communion, Participation, Mission; Final Document" (October 26, 2024) 55.

ualism, which the Church has also often absorbed, and it calls us to mutual care, interdependence and co-responsibility for the common good" ("For a Synodal Church" 48).

Pope Francis himself advanced the ancient practice of synodality in ways that signal a comfortability, if not preference, for organizing as a way of serving the church's mission in a suffering world and divided church. Consider a significant number of Pope Francis "firsts" in the "Synod on Synodality," which underscore the concrete connections between Catholic Social Teaching and the organizing practices we've examined in this book:

- He asked that *all* of the people of God be included in the listening phase of the synod, resulting in what some have called the largest listening campaign in human history.

- He created regional groupings of the world's episcopal conferences (the national conferences of bishops) in order to better identify local priorities that emerged from the global listening campaign. This encouraged an entirely new form of ecclesial subsidiarity.

- He required voting members of the General Assembly of Bishops to use "conversations in the Spirit," the same method of discernment employed by the people of God around the world. This both honored human dignity by holding equal space for delegates to share stories and built the collective power of that body.

- He extended voting status in a General Assembly of Bishops to people other than bishops, which deepened the hierarchy's solidarity with lay and religious women, with lay men and priests. This cultivated the indigenous leadership of delegates who either represented or accompanied marginalized populations and modeled a "power with" approach to authority opposed to a far more familiar power over approach.

- He allowed the recommendations of that deliberative body to stand as the final word on the three-year process, which framed the General Assembly as a kind of public action that witnessed to what might be possible in a church that functions by prioritizing relationship over ideology or doctrine or rank, listening and learning over managing and teaching, and protagonism anchored in baptism over clericalism that privileges holy orders.

- He agreed with synod delegates that cultivating co-responsibility for serving the mission of the church is crucial if we want to bring the many resources of our tradition to the many crises facing our planet.

Echoing models of the church put forward during Vatican II, synod delegates note: "The Church's vocation and its prophetic service consist in witnessing to God's plan to unite all humanity to Himself in freedom and communion . . . It, therefore, walks together with all humanity, strongly committed to justice and peace, human dignity and the common good" ("For a Synodal Church" 20). In short the Synod on Communion, Participation, and Mission was a lesson in community organizing anchored in Catholic Social Teaching.

From Synod to Synodality—Community Organizers as Ministers in a Synodal Church

In his closing homily of the "Synod on Synodality" on the story of Jesus listening to and then healing the blind man, Bartimaeus, Pope Francis commissioned members of the church to listen for Christ, to listen to each other, and then to start walking together along "the Way":

> Brothers and sisters, not a seated Church, but a Church on her feet. Not a silent Church, but a Church that embraces the cry of humanity. Not a blind Church, but a Church, enlightened by Christ, that brings the light of the Gospel to others.

Not a static Church, but a missionary Church that walks with her Lord through the streets of the world.[4]

This particular synod may have formally ended, but the work of becoming a more synodal church has only just begun. Those who seek to integrate the spiritual practices of listening, dialogue, and communal discernment it hopes to catalyze throughout the church will experience similar challenges faced by those who attempt to integrate the principles of CST into the way we are church. Just as CST remains "the church's best kept secret," synodality has been unevenly received, particularly in the US. Commitments to both continues to depend upon the appetite of individual bishops and pastors. We see evidence of the marginalization of CST and sporadic engagement with synodality in the wake of the polarizing 2024 presidential election in which white Christian nationalism successfully fueled xenophobia and other positions that contradict the gospel and principles of Catholic Social Teaching. Rather, perhaps it is an invitation of the Holy Spirit to consider synodality as a method for facing and responding to the unsettling questions the campaigns and election results raise for all of us. Can Catholic Social Teaching, as it is currently presented, sufficiently form the consciences of Catholic voters? Does the Catholic public witness to the values of the gospel have integrity in our polarized political environment? Are US Catholics capable of transcending the tribalism that is fracturing us and shredding the common good?

And yet, after three years of sharing and telling stories, listening for the Holy Spirit to lead participants through conflict and building relationships of trust across various things that otherwise provoke fear, there is ample evidence that synodality provides some guidelines to people of good will for moving forward together in

---

[4] Francis, homily, Conclusion of Ordinary Assembly of Bishops, October 27, 2024.

being co-responsible for mission. When we consider in the delegates' definition of synodality the interplay of personal conversion through encounters with others and structural change through building collective power, we can see that synodality echoes the dynamism of community organizing as a model for justice: "Synodality is a path of spiritual renewal and structural reform that enables the Church to be more participatory in mission, so that it can walk with every man and woman, radiating the light of Christ" ("For a Synodal Church" 28).

We wrote this concluding chapter at an auspicious time in the church's history. The unprecedented Synod on Synodality has concluded and the work of becoming a synodal church in an unprecedentedly fractured church begins. On what would be his final Easter Sunday address, Pope Francis reminded the world "to hope anew and to revive our trust in others";[5] and just weeks later his successor, Pope Leo XIV, whose name invokes the very tradition we've examined in this book, greeted the world with peace and the desire to be "a synodal Church, a Church that moves forward, a Church that always seeks peace, that always seeks charity, that always seeks to be close above all to those who are suffering."[6] Certainly, we'll spend the next generation learning what it means to become a synodal church, and more importantly how to do so in our polarized climate in the US using the tools of our social tradition.

Catholics around the world suggested that becoming a more synodal church, one in which we are all co-responsible for mission, requires ongoing formation in Catholic Social Teaching in order "for the Church to be more confident in contributing to debate and action for justice in the public sphere."[7] In synodal consultations in dioceses across the country, US Catholics indicated a desire for this kind of formation too. "The need for ongoing for-

---

[5] Pope Francis, "'Urbi et Orbi' Message of His Holiness," April 20, 2025.

[6] Pope Leo XIV, "First Blessing 'Urbi et Orbi' of His Holiness," May 8, 2025.

[7] General Secretariat of the Synod, " 'Enlarge the Space of Your Tent' (Is 54:2): Working Document for the Continental Stage" (October 2022) 46.

mation was keenly seen in the area of social mission," the USCCB shared in their 2022 synthesis report at the conclusion of the listening phase: "The Church needs to help parishioners understand the connection between Catholic social teaching and outreach beyond the borders of the parish."[8]

This will be sacred work. Insisting on and modeling relationship as the most central feature of a discipleship that seeks the full flourishing of all of God's creation will be a critical ministry in a church that seeks to follow the protagonism of those on its margins. "We have become aware that the salvation to be received and proclaimed is inherently relational," synod delegates concluded. "We live it and we witness to it together" ("For a Synodal Church" 154).

We'll need community organizers, informed by Catholic Social Teaching, to make this relational salvation happen. We will need community organizers—those who know how to build trust and protagonism through active listening, those who know how to guide people with diverse self-interests through consensus based decision-making processes, those who know how to agitate leaders to relate to their people with greater accountability, those who know how to unleash ecumenical and interfaith commitments to the common good—to live as the lynchpins between our more than a century-old Catholic Social Tradition and the generational project of becoming a more relational church now underway.

Fortunately, delegates to the first General Assembly of Bishops that extended voting status to members of the church other than bishops offer recommendations—some might even say mandates, given the magisterial authority of their final document—for how community organizers can continue to lean into Catholic Social Teaching in ministering to a church that seeks to become co-responsible for mission. To that end, community organizing can

---

[8] USCCB, "National Synthesis of the People of God in the United States of America for the Diocesan Phase of the 2021–2023 Synod" (September 2022), 10. See also Phyllis Zagano, *Just Church: Catholic Social Teaching, Synodality, and Women* (Mahwah, NJ: Paulist Press, 2023).

animate three aspects of synodality that the delegates themselves experienced in their historically unprecedented work together and which shape their own understanding of this ancient and yet emerging way of being and doing church: style, structure, and events ("For a Synodal Church" 31).

Style

If synodality is to become the "*modus vivendi et operandi*" (way of living and functioning) for the church, then community organizers can enhance the deep relationality this will require. As we have seen throughout these chapters, when we foreground our stories and listen for the truth in them, we build relationships of trust among people who are otherwise increasingly disconnected from each other. When we privilege the wisdom of those closest to the pain of the world's problems, we cultivate indigenous leadership that can guide us to solutions we've not yet considered. When we integrate our religious traditions into our search for the common good, we grow a sense of communion in and beyond our own Catholic communities. When we commit ourselves to walking together with others in seeking a more inclusive common good, we engage in deeply spiritual practices akin to synodality itself. "Ecclesial discernment is not an organizational technique," synod delegates explain, "but rather a spiritual practice grounded in a living faith. It calls for interior freedom, humility, prayer, mutual trust, and openness to the new and surrender to the will of God" ("For a Synodal Church" 82). Organizers know how to create conditions for this style of being church together and how to invite others to it.

For example, the three-year Synod on Synodality is a global example of what some have called the largest listening campaign in human history. Catholics around the world gathered in small groups in parish halls, school gyms, and Zoom breakout rooms to share their joys and challenges of journeying with the church. Notetakers captured what was shared and teams drafted synthesis reports that were submitted to church leadership in dioceses and episcopal conferences around the world. A final synthesis report issued from the Vatican in November 2022 captured the faithful's priorities for transforming the church: women's full participation in the church, the need to heal wounds of clergy sexual abuse, the persistent legacy of racism and colonialism, and the need to make a preferential option for young people, to name a few (see "Enlarge the Space of Your Tent"). In their final document, "For a Synodal Church," delegates to the Synod on Synodality recommend "mutual listening, dialogue, and communal discernment," as the central characteristics of a church oriented to serving the gospel (28). "Listening," they note, "is a fundamental element of the path to healing, repentance, justice and reconciliation" (55).

Structure

If synodality is to be more than just conversation, then it needs to reform institutional structures and processes at every level of the church in order to enhance the participation of all of the baptized, as well as people of good will, in discerning the Holy Spirit's promptings and leading the people of God toward the common good. Since community organizers catalyze structural change by transforming how power is exercised in communities, then surely Catholic community organizing can contribute to the church's own conversion away from clericalism, where power is exercised over the laity by those who have received holy orders, toward ecclesial subsidiarity, where power is exercised for and with all who are baptized in the Holy Spirit. "The way to promote a synodal Church," explain synod delegates in "For a Synodal Church," "is to foster greater participation of the People of God in decision-making processes" (87). They note, "The more everyone is heard, the greater the discernment. Therefore, it is essential that we promote the broadest participation possible in the discernment process, particularly involving those who are on the margins of the Christian community and society" (82).

Synodality reflects the historical association of subsidiarity with a call to and right of people to participate in the public life of communities, in this case Catholic communities at every level of the church. It encourages all of the baptized to accept co-responsibility for the mission of the church and to bring their unique individual and collective gifts to that shared project. Delegates to the Synod on Communion, Participation, and Mission have implicitly invoked Pope Pius XI's original intention in 1931 that subsidiarity protect the impulse towards associations and affiliations in an increasingly fractured society. In the synthesis report of the XVI Ordinary General Assembly of Bishops, the first to exercise ecclesial subsidiarity by including non-bishops in the discernment, delegates noted:

> Lay associations, ecclesial movements and new communities are a precious sign of the maturation of the co-responsibility of all the baptized. They hold particular value because of their experience in promoting communion among different vocations, the impetus with which they proclaim the Gospel, their proximity to those on the margins economically and socially and through their promotion of the common good.[9]

Community organizers can assist all of the baptized in understanding this participatory discernment as a kind of "ecclesial subsidiarity." "The primary responsibility for the realization of the individual Christian vocation and the fulfillment of the mission of local churches lies with those individuals and local churches themselves," explains ecclesiologist Richard Gaillardetz in defining this concept. "Only when the realization of these goals appears unattainable at the lower level and/or a local matter threatens the faith and unity of the church universal should there be intervention from higher levels of church authority."[10] In other words,

---

[9] XVI Ordinary General Assembly of the Synod of Bishops, first session, "A Synodal Church in Mission" (October 4–29, 2023), chap. 10.c.

[10] Gaillardetz, "Synodality and the Francis Pontificate," 58.

ecclesial subsidiarity reserves decision-making about how to best serve the mission of the church for the local church—the conference of bishops, the diocese, and even the parish, so long as it unfolds in a process of communal discernment. With our methods of exercising the principle of subsidiarity, community organizers can assist the people of God in discovering and exercising this principle in order to reform how authority is exercised among the people of God, and to grow trust, transparency, and accountability. We will need organizers to help live into recommendations for consultative processes between bishops and their people, for consensus models of decision-making, and for shedding the inertia of internalized clericalism or the sense that those with holy orders are primarily responsible for the church's mission, which keeps Catholics on the sidelines of their faith communities.

Events

If synodality is a public spiritual practice through which we experience our collective power in discerning how we are being called to walk together, particularly through tension and conflict, and receiving gifts from the Holy Spirit that enable us to take next steps together, then community organizers have much to offer about the art of gathering the people. Whether through listening campaigns, research action meetings, or public actions, organizers understand how to help members of a community recognize and amplify their own efficacy for making change, especially through relationships with those at different levels of power. "[Synodality's] orientation is towards mission, and its practice involves gathering in assembly at each level of ecclesial life. It involves reciprocal listening, dialogue, community discernment, and creation of consensus as an expression that renders Christ present in the Holy Spirit, each taking decisions in accordance with their responsibilities."[11] A community

---

[11] "Synodal Church in Mission," chap. 1.h.

organizing approach to the ecclesial assemblies, which synod delegates are calling for at every level of the church, will ensure that Catholic participants, as well as those from other Christian denominations and religious traditions, experience the good of being in relationship and of working with others toward a shared vision, through gatherings grounded in sacred stories and oriented toward the common good.

"Part of the audacity of synodality is that normal baptized people are conduits of the Holy Spirit in their community," explains Leah, the organizer from Minnesota, who helped create pathways of participation in the synod process for thousands of Catholics across the US. "We need our decision-makers to be in rooms with them and consult with them. They have opened up the decision-making processes and now we figure out how decision-makers can walk with everybody in making their decisions. That's the whole business. We become synodal by doing it."[12]

Conclusion

The Holy Spirit continues to reveal the common denominator between Catholic Social Teaching, synodality, and community organizing: relationship. "What emerged throughout the entire synodal journey, in every place and context, was the call for a Church with greater capacity to nurture relationships: with the Lord, between men and women, in the family, in the local community, among social groups and religions, with the earth itself" ("For a Synodal Church" 50).

Community organizers steeped in Catholic Social Teaching know how to nurture these kinds of relationships for the sake of serving the church's mission. May the people of good will follow their lead as we continue to walk together on the way of Jesus.

---

[12] Interview with Leah, November 12, 2024.

Acknowledgments

These principles of Catholic Social Teaching and practices of organizing come to life through stories from community organizers who contributed to the book. We are especially grateful to Annie Fox, Kathleen Maas Weigert, Lorena Melgarejo, Joseph McKeller, Joseph Fleming, Tracey Horan, Rose Lue, Ken Homan, Paul Maricel, and Terri Bergen. Many of these organizers came together in February 2023 at the University of San Francisco for a conference on community organizing and Catholic Social Teaching entitled "Prophetic Communities." We want to acknowledge all the speakers and organizers of the conference as well as the Catholic Collaborative for Community Organizing, which emerged from that gathering. We also want to thank Bill Purcell, who inspired many students and practitioners of Catholic Social Teaching during his tenure at the Institute for Social Concerns, and Connie Mick, who generously guided us in the writing of this book.

Appendix

Semi-Structured Interview Questions:

Personal Story Questions (getting at the who and the why of the particular organizer)

- What motivates you as a community organizer? / Why are you a community organizer?
- Who are your people? Where / How are you trying to move them?
- What aspect of your faith most speaks to or supports you in your vocation as a community organizer?
- What model of church or image of church speaks to you or you see in action as an organizer?
- What impact did Pope Francis's leadership and witness have on you as an organizer? What impact did it have on your people?
- Does being a Catholic make any difference for you as an organizer?

Organizing Questions (illuminating essential elements of community organizing)

- Can you tell us an organizing story that stands out to you?

- What do you think makes community organizing a distinct method of justice (as opposed to direct service or even advocacy or activism?)
  - Can you give us a concrete example of where you have seen this in action?
- What contributions do Catholic community organizers offer/bring to the church?
- What do you think are the most critical skills a community organizer possesses or uses?
  - Can you give us a concrete example of where you have seen this in action?
- What distinct contributions, if any, do Catholics (or Catholicism) make to community organizing where you are?

Catholic Social Teaching Questions (revealing points of convergence, areas for deepening alignment)

- What principle(s) of CST inspire you the most? Why?
- What principles of CST do you see in action on a regular basis?
  - Can you give us a concrete example?
- What would you recommend we do in order to convert Catholic Social Teaching from "our best kept secret" to our "favorite recipe for building the kingdom of God"?

Bibliography

XVI Ordinary General Assembly of the Synod of Bishops. First Session. "A Synodal Church in Mission." October 4–29, 2023. https://www.synod.va/content/dam/synod/assembly/synthesis/english/2023.10.28-ENG-Synthesis-Report.pdf.

XVI Ordinary General Assembly of the Synod of Bishops. Second Session. "For a Synodal Church: Communion, Participation, Mission; Final Document." October 26, 2024. https://www.usccb.org/resources/ENG---Documento-finale_traduzione-di-lavoro.pdf.

Alinsky, Saul D. *Reveille for Radicals*. Chicago: University of Chicago Press, 1945.

Alinsky, Saul D. *Rules for Radicals: A Practical Primer for Realistic Radicals*. New York: Vintage Books, 1972.

Beyer, Gerald J. "The Meaning of Solidarity in Catholic Social Teaching." *Political Theology* 15, no. 1 (2014): 7–25.

Bretherton, Luke. *Christ and the Common Life: Political Theology and the Case for Democracy*. Grand Rapids, MI: Eerdmans, 2019.

Bretherton, Luke. *Resurrecting Democracy: Faith, Citizenship, and the Politics of a Common Life*. New York: Cambridge University Press, 2015.

Buckeye, Jeanne. "Exploring Subsidiarity: The Case of the Economy of Communion." *Journal of Religion and Society*, supplement 22 (2020).

Chambers, Edward T. *Roots for Radicals: Organizing for Power, Action, and Justice*. 2nd ed. New York: Continuum, 2018.

Clark, Meghan J. "Anatomy of a Social Virtue: Solidarity and Corresponding Vices." *Political Theology* 15, no. 1 (2014): 26–39.

Clark, Meghan J. "Pope Francis and the Christological Dimensions of Solidarity in Catholic Social Teaching." *Theological Studies* 80, no. 1 (March 2019): 102–22.

Dávila, María Teresa. "Building a Church of Liberation: Orthopraxis as the Public Shape of the Church's Common Good." *Journal of the Society of Christian Ethics* 42, no. 2 (2022): 265–72.

Dorr, Donal. *Option for the Poor and for the Earth.* Maryknoll, NY: Orbis Books, 2016.

Engel, Lawrence J. "The Influence of Saul Alinsky on the Campaign for Human Development." *Theological Studies* 59, no. 4 (December 1998): 636–61.

Engh, Susan. *Women's Work: The Transformational Power of Faith-Based Community Organizing.* Lanham, MD: Lexington Books/Fortress Academic, 2019.

Farley, Margaret. *Personal Commitments: Beginning, Keeping, Changing.* Maryknoll, NY: Orbis Books, 2013.

Finks, P. David. *The Radical Vision of Saul Alinsky.* Mahwah, NJ: Paulist Press, 1984.

Fulton, Brad R., and Marc Doussard. "Sustaining the Grassroots: How Community Organizations Mitigate the Downsides of Collaborating with Unions." *Journal of Urban Affairs* 45, no. 4 (2021): 835–54.

Fulton, Brad R., Michelle Oyakawa, and Richard L. Wood. "Critical Standpoint: Leaders of Color Advancing Racial Equality in Predominantly White Organizations." *Nonprofit Management & Leadership* 30, no. 2 (Winter 2019): 255–76. doi:10.1002/nml.21387.

Gaillardetz, Richard. "Synodality and the Francis Pontificate: A Fresh Reception of Vatican II." *Theological Studies* 84, no. 1 (March 2023): 44–60.

Ganz, Marshall. *Leadership, Organizing, and Action: SEED Organizing Workshop Participant Guide.* Cambridge, MA, August 7–9, 2015. https://projects.iq.harvard.edu/files/ganzorganizing/files/seed_organizing_manual_final_2015_ok_coaching_appendix.pdf.

Ganz, Marshall. *People, Power, Change: Organizing for Democratic Renewal.* New York: Oxford University Press, 2024.

Ganz, Marshall. "What Is Public Narrative: Self, Us and Now" (Public Narrative Worksheet—Working Paper). 2009. https://leading changenetwork.org/resource_center/what-is-public-narrative-self-us-and-now-public-narrative-worksheet-working-paper/.

Ganz, Marshall. *Why David Sometimes Wins: Leadership, Organization, and Strategy in the California Farm Worker Movement.* New York: Oxford University Press, 2009.

General Secretariat of the Synod. "'Enlarge the Space of Your Tent' (Is 54:2): Working Document for the Continental Stage." October 2022. https://www.synod.va/content/dam/synod/common/phases/continental-stage/dcs/Documento-Tappa-Continentale-EN.pdf.

Gutiérrez, Gustavo. *A Theology of Liberation: History, Politics, and Salvation.* Rev. ed. Maryknoll, NY: Orbis Books, 1988.

Hak, Joon Lee. *God and Community Organizing: A Covenantal Approach.* Waco, TX: Baylor University Press, 2020.

Harvard University. The Pluralism Project. "From Diversity to Pluralism." 2020. https://pluralism.org/from-diversity-to-pluralism.

Hayes-Mota, Nicholas. "An Accountable Church? Broad-Based Community Organizing and Ecclesial Ethics." *Journal of the Society of Christian Ethics* 43, no. 1 (Spring–Summer, 2023): 111–28.

Hayes-Mota, Nicholas. "Embodying the Common Good: Community Organizing as Practice and Tradition." *The Journal of Catholic Social Thought* 21, no. 2 (2024).

Hickey, Kelli Reagan, and Clemens Sedmak. *Counting the Cost: Financial Decision-Making, Discipleship, and Christian Living,* Collegeville, MN: Liturgical Press, 2023.

Hinze, Bradford E. *Prophetic Obedience: Ecclesiology for a Dialogical Church.* Maryknoll, NY: Orbis Books, 2016.

Hinze, Bradford E. "Vatican II and U.S. Catholic Communities: Promoting Grassroots Democracy." In *The Legacy of Vatican II*, edited by Massimo Faggioli and Andrea Vicini, SJ, 152–81. Mahwah, NJ: Paulist Press, 2015.

Hollenbach, David. *The Common Good and Christian Ethics.* New York: Cambridge University Press, 2002.

Jacobsen, Dennis A. *Doing Justice: Congregations and Community Organizing.* Minneapolis: Fortress Press, 2001.

Krier Mich, Marvin. *Catholic Social Teaching and Movements.* Mystic, CT: Twenty-Third Publications, 1998, 6th printing 2006.

Linthicum, Robert. *Transforming Power: Biblical Strategies for Making a Difference in Your Community.* Downers Grove, IL: InterVarsity Press, 2003.

Maas Weigert, Kathleen, and Alexia Kelley, eds. *Living the Catholic Social Tradition: Cases and Commentary.* Lanham, MD: Rowman & Littlefield, 2005.

Mulligan, Suzanne. *Dwelling with Dignity: Catholic Social Teaching and Homelessness.* Collegeville, MN: Liturgical Press, 2025.

Ozzano, Luca, and Sara Fenoglio. "Conceptions of Power and Role of Religion in Community Organising." *Religions* 13, no. 9 (2022): 1–16.

Pontifical Council for Justice and Peace. *Compendium of the Social Doctrine of the Church.* Washington, DC: USCCB Publishing, 2005.

Pope Benedict XVI. *Caritas in Veritate.* Vatican, June 29, 2009. https://www.vatican.va/content/benedict-xvi/en/encyclicals/documents/hf_ben-xvi_enc_20090629_caritas-in-veritate.html.

Pope Benedict XVI. *Deus Caritas Est.* Vatican, December 25, 2005. https://www.vatican.va/content/benedict-xvi/en/encyclicals/documents/hf_ben-xvi_enc_20051225_deus-caritas-est.html.

Pope Francis. Address of His Holiness Pope Francis for the Opening of the Synod, New Synod Hall, Holy See. October 9, 2021. https://www.vatican.va/content/francesco/en/speeches/2021/october/documents/20211009-apertura-camminosinodale.html.

Pope Francis. Address of Pope Francis to the Participants in the World Meeting of Popular Movements. Holy See, October 28, 2014. https://www.vatican.va/content/francesco/en/speeches/2014/october/documents/papa-francesco_20141028_incontro-mondiale-movimenti-popolari.html.

Pope Francis. Address of the Holy Father, Participation at the Second World Meeting of Popular Movements. Holy See, July 9, 2015. https://www.vatican.va/content/francesco/en/speeches/2015/july

/documents/papa-francesco_20150709_bolivia-movimenti-popolari.html.

Pope Francis. *Evangelii Gaudium*. Vatican, November 24, 2013. https://www.vatican.va/content/francesco/en/apost_exhortations/documents/papa-francesco_esortazione-ap_20131124_evangelii-gaudium.html.

Pope Francis. *Fratelli Tutti*. Vatican, October 3, 2020. https://www.vatican.va/content/francesco/en/encyclicals/documents/papa-francesco_20201003_enciclica-fratelli-tutti.html.

Pope Francis. General Audience. September 23, 2020. https://www.vatican.va/content/francesco/en/audiences/2020/documents/papa-francesco_20200923_udienza-generale.html.

Pope Francis. Homily of Holy Father Francis. Visit to Lampedusa. July 8, 2013. https://www.vatican.va/content/francesco/en/homilies/2013/documents/papa-francesco_20130708_omelia-lampedusa.html.

Pope Francis. Homily of the Holy Father Francis. Conclusion of the Ordinary General Assembly of the Synod of Bishops. October 27, 2024. https://www.vatican.va/content/francesco/en/homilies/2024/documents/20241027-omelia-conclusione-sinodo.html.

Pope Francis. *Laudato Si'*. Vatican, May 24, 2015. https://www.vatican.va/content/francesco/en/encyclicals/documents/papa-francesco_20150524_enciclica-laudato-si.html.

Pope Francis. Message of His Holiness Pope Francis on the Occasion of the World Meeting of Popular Movements in Modesto. Holy See, February 10, 2017. https://www.vatican.va/content/francesco/en/messages/pont-messages/2017/documents/papa-francesco_20170210_movimenti-popolari-modesto.html.

Pope Francis. "Urbi et Orbi" Message of His Holiness Pope Francis. Holy See, April 20, 2025. https://www.vatican.va/content/francesco/en/messages/urbi/documents/20250420-urbi-et-orbi-pasqua.html.

Pope Francis. Video Message of the Holy Father Francis on the Occasion of the Fourth World Meeting of Popular Movements. Holy See, October 16, 2021. https://www.vatican.va/content/francesco/en/messages/pont-messages/2021/documents/20211016-videomessaggio-movimentipopolari.html.

Pope Francis and Austen Ivereigh. *Let Us Dream: The Path to a Better Future*. New York: Simon & Schuster, 2020.

Pope John XXIII. *Mater et Magistra*. Vatican, May 15, 1961. https://www.vatican.va/content/john-xxiii/en/encyclicals/documents/hf_j-xxiii_enc_15051961_mater.html.

Pope John XXIII. *Pacem in Terris*. Vatican, April 11, 1963. https://www.vatican.va/content/john-xxiii/en/encyclicals/documents/hf_j-xxiii_enc_11041963_pacem.html.

Pope John Paul II. *Centesimus Annus*. Vatican, May 1, 1991. https://www.vatican.va/content/john-paul-ii/en/encyclicals/documents/hf_jp-ii_enc_01051991_centesimus-annus.html.

Pope John Paul II. *Laborem Exercens*. Vatican, September 14, 1981. https:// www.vatican.va/content/john-paul-ii/en/encyclicals/documents/hf_jp-ii_enc_14091981_laborem-exercens.html.

Pope John Paul II. *Sollicitudo Rei Socialis*. Vatican, December 30, 1987. https://www.vatican.va/content/john-paul-ii/en/encyclicals/documents/hf_jp-ii_enc_30121987_sollicitudo-rei-socialis.html.

Pope Leo XIII. *Rerum Novarum*. Vatican, 1891. https://www.vatican.va/content/leo-xiii/en/encyclicals/documents/hf_l-xiii_enc_15051891_rerum-novarum.html.

Pope Leo XIV. First Blessing "Urbi et Orbi" of His Holiness Pope Leo XIV. Holy See, May 8, 2025. https://www.vatican.va/content/leo-xiv/en/messages/urbi/documents/20250508-prima-benedizione-urbietorbi.html.

Pope Paul VI. *Gaudium et Spes*. December 7, 1965. In *Vatican Council II: Constitutions, Decrees, Declarations; The Basic Sixteen Documents*, edited by Austin Flannery. Collegeville, MN: Liturgical Press, 2014.

Pope Paul VI. *Octogesima Adveniens*. Vatican, May 14, 1971. https://www.vatican.va/content/paul-vi/en/apost_letters/documents/hf_p-vi_apl_19710514_octogesima-adveniens.html.

Pope Paul VI. *Populorum Progressio*. Vatican, March 6, 1967. https://www.vatican.va/content/paul-vi/en/encyclicals/documents/hf_p-vi_enc_26031967_populorum.html.

Pope Pius XI. *Quadragesimo Anno.* Vatican, May 15, 1931. https://www.vatican.va/content/pius-xi/en/encyclicals/documents/hf_p-xi_enc_19310515_quadragesimo-anno.html.

Regan, Ethna. "The Bergoglian Principles: Pope Francis' Dialectical Approach to Political Theology." *Religions* 10, no. 12 (2019).

Rowlands, Anna. *Towards a Politics of Communion: Catholic Social Teaching in Dark Times.* London: T&T Clark, 2021.

Salvatierra, Alexia. "Latinx Missiology and Faith-Rooted Organizing: Poder Espiritual y Justicia Social." *Journal of Religious Leadership* 18, no. 2 (2019): 85–106.

Scannone, Juan Carlos. "Pope Francis and the Theology of the People." *Theological Studies* 77, no. 1 (March 2016).

Scott, Katie Collins. "For Synod Listening Sessions, US Bishops Turned to Community Organizers." *National Catholic Reporter.* January 3, 2023.

Secretary General of the Synod of Bishops. "Official Handbook for Listening and Discernment in Local Churches: First Phase, October 2021–April 2022." September 2021. https://www.synod.va/content/dam/synod/common/vademecum/en_vade.pdf.

Secretary General of the Synod of Bishops. "The Spiritual Conversation." 2021. https://www.synod.va/content/dam/synod/common/phases/en/EN_Step_6_Spiritual-Conversation.pdf.

Spadaro, SJ, Antonio. Interview with Pope Francis. "A Big Heart Open to God." *America.* September 19, 2013.

Speer, Paul W., and Hahrie Han. "Re-Engaging Social Relationships and Collective Dimensions of Organizing to Revive Democratic Practice." *Journal of Social and Political Psychology* 6, no. 2 (2018).

Stauffer, Aaron. *Listening to the Spirit: The Radical Social Gospel, Sacred Value, and Broad-Based Community Organizing.* New York: Oxford University Press, 2024.

Stauffer, Aaron. "The Relational Meeting as a Political and Religious Practice." *Political Theology* 23, nos. 1–2 (2022): 167–73.

Stout, Jeffrey. *Blessed Are the Organized: Grassroots Democracy in America.* Princeton, NJ: Princeton University Press, 2010.

United States Catholic Bishops. "Economic Justice for All: Pastoral Letter on Catholic Social Teaching and the U.S. Economy." 1986. https://www.usccb.org/upload/economic_justice_for_all.pdf.

United States Catholic Bishops. "Seven Themes of Catholic Social Teaching," drawn from *Sharing Catholic Social Teaching: Challenges and Directions*. Washington, DC: USCCB Publishing, 1998.

United States Conference of Catholic Bishops. "National Synthesis of the People of God in the United States of America for the Diocesan Phase of the 2021–2023 Synod." September 2022. https://www.usccb.org/resources/US%20National%20Synthesis%202021-2023%20Synod.pdf.

Verhey, Allen Dale. *The Great Reversal: Ethics and the New Testament*. Grand Rapids, MI: Eerdmans, 1984.

Vogt, Christopher. "Fostering a Catholic Commitment to the Common Good: An Approach Rooted in Virtue Ethics." *Theological Studies* 68, no. 2 (May 2007).

Whitman, Gordon. *Stand Up! How to Get Involved, Speak Out, and Win in a World on Fire*. Oakland, CA: Berrett-Koehler, 2017.

Wood, Richard L. *Faith in Action: Religion, Race, and Democratic Organizing in America*. Chicago: University of Chicago Press, 2002.

Wood, Richard L. "Public Catholicism: Contemporary Presence and Future Promise." In *The Future of Catholicism in America*, edited by Patricia O'Connell Killen and Mark Silk. New York: Columbia University Press, 2019.

Wood, Richard L., and Brad R. Fulton. *A Shared Future: Faith-Based Organizing for Racial Equity and Ethical Democracy*. Chicago: University of Chicago Press, 2015.

World Synod of Catholic Bishops. "Justice in the World." Vatican, 1971. https://educationforjustice.org/wp-content/uploads/2007/09/justiciainmundo.pdf.